Hands-On ALPHABET ACTIVITIES

—for— YOUNG CHILDREN

A Whole Language Plus Phonics Approach to Reading

ROBERTA SECKLER BROWN & SUSAN CAREY

Family Education Network
Pearson
Boston, Massachusetts 02116

Library of Congress Cataloging-in-Publication Data

Brown, Roberta Seckler.
    Hands-on alphabet activities for young children : a whole language
plus phonics approach to reading / Roberta Seckler Brown & Susan
Carey.
      p.   cm.
    Includes bibliographical references.
    ISBN 0–87628–394–6 (spiral)   ISBN 0–87628–390–3 (paper)
     1. Reading—Language experience approach—Handbooks, manuals, etc.
2. Reading—Phonetic method—Handbooks, manuals, etc.   3. Reading
(Early childhood education)—Handbooks, manuals, etc.   4. Reading
readiness—Handbooks, manuals, etc.   5. English language—Alphabet—
Study and teaching (Early childhood)   6. Early childhood education—
Activity programs—Handbooks, manuals, etc.   I. Carey, Susan.
II. Title.
LB1050.35.B76   1995
372.4'14—dc20   94–45840
                                               CIP

Printed in the United States of America

10 9 8 7   *(spiral wire)*   *10 9 8*   *VOCR*   *(paper)*

ISBN 0-87628-394-6 (spiral wire)   ISBN 0-87628-390-3 (paper)

Family Education Network
Pearson
Boston, Massachusetts 02116

Dedication

We wish to dedicate this book to our families and all of the children who have touched our lives.

Acknowledgments

Many thanks to the following people for their time, expertise, and encouragement; Christopher Brown–photographer, Joanie Cioffi–typist extraordinaire, Elizabeth Kavanaugh and Barney Carpfinger–for their valuable advice. And fellow authors, mentors, and friends–Chris Heath, Jean Grasso Fitzpatrick, and Sam Freedman.

About the Authors

ROBERTA SECKLER BROWN received her B.A. from Fordham University and her master's degree as a reading specialist from St. John's University. Mrs. Brown is also certified from New York University as a Reading Recovery teacher.

SUSAN CAREY received her B.S. from the State University College of New York at Brockport and her master's degree in early childhood education from Western Connecticut University. Mrs. Carey is also certified from New York University as a Reading Recovery teacher.

The authors have two children's books included in Scholastic Inc.'s Wiggle Works Reading Program: *Hide and Seek* and *The Tree House.*

Sue and Roberta are educational consultants who present reading workshops to educators and are currently teaching Kindergarten and Reading Recovery at the Park Early Childhood Center for the Ossining Public Schools, Ossining, New York.

About This Book

Hands-On Alphabet Activities for Young Children is a Reading Readiness program that bridges the gap between whole language and more traditional phonetic approaches by providing young children with "real" reading experiences as they master the letters and sounds of the alphabet. Early childhood, reading, resource room, and special education teachers can use the program for whole group and individualized instruction.

This unique resource uses poems, big books, and a series of individual "little letter books" that are written for each letter of the alphabet. Children are taught letters-sounds and book-handling knowledge through immersion in real reading experiences. From the beginning of the program, children are *reading* poems and books that are engaging yet challenging.

Included in the easy-to-follow lessons for each letter of the alphabet are:

- an objective for the day
- materials needed
- an introduction
- specific directions
- an art activity

- independent activity
- individualized instruction
- a lesson summary
- bibliography (pages 509-514)
- reproducible blackline masters

By actively involving students in book-handling experiences and letter-sound awareness, *Hands-On Alphabet Activities for Young Children* builds self-esteem and increases independence:

Book-Handling—Through hands-on reading, children learn directionality, one-to-one correspondence, and that meaning is derived from text.

Letter-Sound Awareness—Each book is based on a letter of the alphabet focusing the children on the sound/symbol relationship.

Self-Esteem—Children are challenged by putting together all the isolated skills they are learning. The reward is successful reading and increased confidence.

Independence—When children become independent readers, they take ownership of their learning. This program gives the responsibility of learning back to the child. Children take ownership and are engaged in two ways. First, the letter books are designed to be consumable. Children color in the illustrations and it becomes their book. Second, the books are predictable and expose children to high frequency words, and thus promote a high accuracy level.

And to encourage parental involvement in the program, a letter is included that can be sent home at the beginning of the school year. The letter explains the program and asks parents to listen to their children read their little letter books when they bring them home.

We've successfully used this program with our own students. We wish you and your students the same success that we've experienced!

Roberta Seckler Brown and Susan Carey

How to Use This Book

Hands-On Alphabet Activities for Young Children is divided into 27 chapters, one for each letter of the alphabet and a final project. Each chapter contains three daily lesson plans and a bibliography of suggested story books. The structure of the lesson plans is consistent throughout the book:

Lesson 1—In the first lesson, children learn to visually recognize the letter by its name and to auditorily recognize it as the initial sound in various words. Blackline masters are provided for a related poem and art activity.

Lesson 2—Next, children reread the poem and then read a big letter book after the teacher models directionality and 1-1 match. For an independent activity, children color the illustrations of their little letter books and then read the predictable story after the teacher models the same procedures again. Blackline masters are included for the big and little letter books.

Lesson 3—Finally, children use specific strategies while reading their little letter books to make sure what they're reading makes sense (meaning) ... determine whether what they read sounds grammatically correct (structure) ... recognize the correct letter as the initial sound when reading a word in context (visual) ... and understand what they read has to match the number of words on a page (1-1 match). A blackline master is included for an award.

After children have successfully read each letter book, an award is pinned to their clothing that reads, "I can read My _____ Book. Just ask me!" To reinforce the importance of this award, you'll find a letter to send home with children at the start of the school year explaining the program and the need to have at least one adult at home listen as the child reads his/her little letter books.

Included in "How to Use This Book" are a reproducible Parent Letter to be sent home at the beginning of the school year and instructions for materials to be made prior to teaching each letter of the alphabet:

1. Letter cans
2. Chart-size poems
3. Big books
4. "Little" letter books
5. Awards

Each chapter includes blackline masters for little books, poems, art activities, and awards.

Hands-On Alphabet Activities for Young Children gives step-by-step instructions on how to teach beginning reading strategies. It focuses children on the four main cueing systems needed to become a successful reader. This is the key to help the child see the connection between phonetic and whole language approaches.

■ **Meaning**   Child must determine if what he/she has read makes sense in relation to a picture and in the context of the book the child is reading.

■ **Visual**   Child will use a letter in the initial position to read a word in context.

■ **Structure**   Child must be able to hear what he/she has read and determine if it sounds right grammatically.

■ **1-to-1 Match**   Child must understand that what he/she says has to match the number of words on a page.

Lesson 3 of each letter includes an individualized instruction component. This is your opportunity to reinforce the four main cueing systems:

As you are reading with students, they will make various reading errors. Also included in Lesson 3 are examples of reading errors, and the "appropriate" teacher responses to correct the errors.

The child's response may not be an exact match to the example. However, if the response is the same type of mistake (meaning, structure, visual, 1-to-1 match), prompt the child with the appropriate question.

Your phrasing of the questions must be consistent with those in the example. After using the appropriate strategy question, if the child still cannot recall the word, tell the child the word! Have the child reread.

Teach the child right from the start that reading is *not* a trick!

September _____

Dear Parents:

My focus this year will be to build your child's self-esteem, confidence, and independence, as well as promoting his/her academic abilities.

I will provide a positive school experience for your child and set a strong foundation for learning. I will apply my knowledge, commitment, and understanding to your child.

I will be using the *Hands-On Alphabet Activities for Young Children,* which provides a unique approach to reading readiness. The program incorporates poems, art activities, and specially designed letter books.

Upon completing the study of each letter of the alphabet and successfully "reading" the little letter book, your child will bring home an award asking you to listen to him/her read.

With your support, we will see your child's enthusiasm for reading come alive!

Here's to a great year!

Sincerely,

Instructions for Making ...

1. LETTER CANS

Materials:

- 26 clean coffee cans (with lids)
- Contact paper
- Black permanent marker
- Scissors

Directions:

1. Cover each coffee can with contact paper.
2. Write a capital and lower case letter on the can.

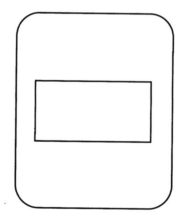

3. Fill the can with the appropriate items for the letter that appears on the outside of the can.

2. CHART-SIZE POEMS

Materials:

- 1 Large, lined piece of chart paper (approximately 3' × 2') for each poem you are making
- Black permanent marker

Directions:

1. Using the "little poem" as a guide, write the poem as it appears.
2. Make sure to leave enough space between lines so the poem does not appear visually confusing.
3. Laminate, if possible.

3. BIG BOOKS

Materials:

▮ 5 - 12" × 18" white pieces of construction paper, for each book you are making

▮ 1- 12" × 18" colored piece of construction paper, for each book cover you are making

▮ Permanent black marker

▮ Stapler

▮ Blackline of big book pictures for the letter book you are making

▮ Crayons or markers (for coloring in blacklines)

▮ Scissors

Directions:

1. Xerox blackline big book pictures for the letter book.
2. Cut out and color the pictures.
3. Placing paper horizontally, glue one picture on each page, 3" from the top and centered.
4. Make sure to leave a 3" margin from the left when you begin writing the words.
5. Using the "little letter book" as a guide, you write with permanent black marker the appropriate words under each picture or use the words supplied on the blackline masters.

4. "LITTLE" LETTER BOOKS

Materials:

▮ Blacklines of the little letter book you are making

▮ Stapler

▮ Paper cutter

Directions:

1. For the little letter book you are making, reproduce one *complete* copy of the blacklines for each child.

2. Cut the pages on the dotted line.

3. Collate pages, making sure the last page is the "surprise ending."

4. Staple along the left side of the book.

5. AWARDS

Materials:

- Blackline of the award you are making
- Scissors
- Permanent marker

Directions:

1. Reproduce one award per child.

2. Cut out award.

3. Using permanent marker, write the child's name on the award.

Contents

Letter Gg   **113**

Letter Hh   **133**

Letter Ii   **151**

Letter Jj 171

Letter Kk 191

Letter Nn   251

Letter Oo   271

Letter Pp   291

Letter Qq   311

Letter Rr   329

Letter Uu
387

Letter Vv
407

Letter Ww
427

LETTER

LESSON 1

Objective:

Child will

▪ visually recognize letter by name.

▪ recognize the sound /a/ in the initial position by naming words with a in that position.

Materials:

▪ Large chart with poem, *Apples* (see directions on p. x)

▪ Any alphabet card with the letter Aa

▪ Letter Aa can, containing such items as:
  – magazine picture of astronaut
  – small bag of alphabet macaroni
  – plastic apple and ape

Procedure:

STEP 1

1. Introduce the lesson with the poem *Apples.*

2. Display the poem on an easel. You read the poem modeling 1-1 match with a pointer.

1

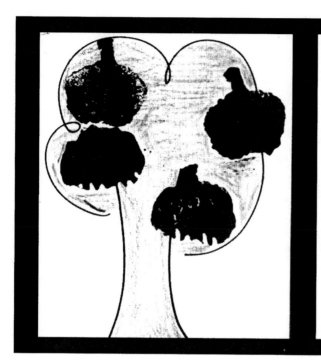

Apples

Apples are so good to eat,
To have one is a special treat.
Red, green, yellow, too,
All of them are good for you!

3. Ask the whole group, "What letter of the alphabet do you think we are studying now?"
4. Ask children to echo read the poem several times.
5. Ask children for suggestions of movements for acting out the poem.
6. Reread the poem together, acting it out!
7. Put the poem aside.

STEP 2

1. Display the alphabet card with the letter Aa.
2. Ask children to name the letter they see on the alphabet card.
3. Hold up the letter Aa can.
4. Ask children to predict what would make sense in an Aa can.
5. Take each object/picture out of the can. Name them.
6. Ask children to repeat the name of each object/picture after you name it.
7. Show children a sample of the art activity.

8. You now do the art activity with the children, either as a small group or whole class.

ART ACTIVITY

Sponge-painted apples

Materials

▪ Blackline master of the poem *Apples*
▪ Blackline master of the apple tree
▪ Crayons
▪ Green construction paper 12″ × 18″
▪ White construction paper 8-1/2″ × 11″
▪ Red paint
▪ Four sponges cut in the shape of apples
▪ Stapler

Preparation:

Reproduce the poem *Apples* and staple it to the right side of the green construction paper.

Procedure:

1. Children color the tree.
2. With teacher guidance, children dip sponges in red paint and press on the tree.
3. Let dry.
4. Staple tree to left side of the green construction paper.
5. Send the poem and art activity home. This gives family members an opportunity to reread the poem with the child, reinforcing the letter Aa.

CONCLUSION OF LESSON

Remind children they have learned to recognize letter Aa and they can think of words that have Aa in the initial position.

Apples

Apples are so good to eat,

To have one is a special treat.

Red, green, yellow, too,

All of them are good for you!

Apples

Apples are so good to eat,

To have one is a special treat.

Red, green, yellow, too,

All of them are good for you!

©1995 by Roberta Seckler Brown and Susan Carey

BLACKLINE MASTER—POEM

4

BLACKLINE MASTER—APPLE TREE

LESSON 2

Objective:

Children will read *My Aa Book* using 1-1 match.

Materials:

- Big Book—*My Aa Book* (see directions p. xi)
- Large poem—*Apples* (see directions p. x)
- Little books—*My Aa Book* (see directions p. xi)
- Crayons

Procedure:

1. Introduce the lesson with the poem *Apples*.
2. You reread the poem *Apples* modeling 1-1 match with a pointer. Children echo read the poem and act it out.
3. You hold up the "big book," *My Aa Book*. You read the title. Children echo read.
4. You go through each page of the "big book," covering all print. You name the picture on the page. Tell the children to listen for Aa words.
5. You read through the "big book" one time, modeling 1-1 match and directionality.
6. Invite the children to now read the "big book" with you. Model 1-1 match and directionality while reading.
7. The children read through the book a third time while you point to the words.

INDEPENDENT ACTIVITY

1. Reproduce blackline master of the little *My Aa Book*. Give children their own little *My Aa Book* and have them color it in.
2. After children color in their own little *My Aa Book,* they read their book to a partner.
3. You monitor the activity, looking for 1-1 match and directionality.
4. Collect the books.

CONCLUSION OF LESSON

1. You gather the whole group back together for whole group instruction.
2. Everyone rereads the "big book," *My Aa Book,* together.
3. While the children are reading the "big book," you model 1-1 match and directionality, while pointing to the words.

My Aa Book

_____
(name)

The astronaut.

The apple.

- -

The alligator.

The ax.

- -

ABCDEFGHIJKLMNOPQRSTUVWXYZ

The alphabet!

F

A B C D E F G H I J K L M N O P Q R S T U V W X Y Z

LESSON 3

Objective:

Child will focus on the 4 main cueing systems while reading little book, *My Aa Book.*

Materials:

▪ Big Book—*My Aa Book*
▪ Little books—*My Aa Book*
▪ Awards (see directions p. xii)
▪ Safety pins

Procedure:

1. Introduce the lesson with the big book, *My Aa Book.*
2. You read the "big book" with the children, modeling 1-1 match and directionality while pointing to the words.
3. Echo read the book.

INDIVIDUALIZED INSTRUCTION

Note—The objective is to focus the child on the 4 main cueing systems:

▪ Meaning
▪ Structure
▪ Visual
▪ 1-1 Match

(See page viii for definition and more information.)

1. You now take each child, one at a time, having him/her read the little book, *My Aa Book,* to you. Child points to words while reading.
2. As the child is reading to you, you are listening for misread text and prompting the child with the appropriate question to help him/her correct the error. Your phrasing of the questions must be consistent with those in "Examples of Misread Text."
3. Through repeated use of these techniques, the children will begin to ask themselves these questions. This indicates the child is now monitoring his/her own reading and is on the way to becoming an independent reader.
4. Following are specific examples of misread text by a child using little *My Aa Book.* Find the type of example that matches what your student has read. After using the appropriate strategy questions and the child still can

not recall the word, then tell the child the word! Teach the child right from the start that reading is *not* a trick!

5. The child's response may not be an exact match to the example. However, if the response is a similar mistake, prompt the child with the appropriate question.

Examples of Misread Text

Following are specific examples of misread text by a child using little *My Aa Book*. Find the type of example that matches what your student has read. Keep in mind that the child's response may not be an exact match to the example. However, if the response is a similar mistake, prompt the child with the appropriate question.

WHEN TO USE MEANING QUESTIONS

Objective:

Child must determine if what he/she has read makes sense in relation to the picture and in the context of the book he/she is reading.

Example

Child reads: The orange.
Text reads: The apple.

Strategy

Teacher: "Look at the picture. Is that an orange?"

Child: "No. It's an apple."

Teacher: "Good! *Good readers reread.*"

WHEN TO USE STRUCTURE QUESTIONS

Objective:

Child must be able to hear what he/she has read and determine if it sounds right grammatically.

Example

Child reads: Then alligator.
Text reads: The alligator.

Strategy

Teacher:	"Does that sound right? Is that how people talk?"
Child:	"No."
Teacher:	"What would sound right?"
Child:	"The alligator."
Teacher:	"Good! *Good readers reread.*"

WHEN TO USE VISUAL QUESTIONS

Objective:

Child will use letter in the initial position to read a word in context.

Example

Child reads: The man.
Text reads: The astronaut.

Strategy

You point to misread word: "What word do you know that starts with letter a and makes sense?"

Child: "Astronaut."

Teacher: "Reread."

If the child hesitates and cannot recall the word, give it! Then have the child reread.

WHEN TO USE 1-1 QUESTIONS

Objective:

Child must understand what he/she says has to match the number of words on the page.

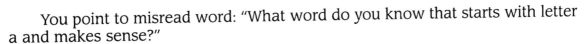

Example 1

Child reads: The letters of the alphabet.
Text reads: The alphabet.

Strategy

Teacher:	"Did your finger match the words?"
Child:	"No."
Teacher:	*"Reread."*

If the finger does not match the second time, you take the child's finger and point to the words together.

Example 2

Child reads:	Ax.
Text reads:	The ax.

Strategy

Teacher:	"Did your finger match the words?"
Child:	*"No."*
Teacher:	"Reread."

If the child responds, "Yes, my finger did match," take the child's finger and point to the words together.

LETTER Aa AWARD

When the child has successfully read his/her own My Aa Book to you, reward the child with an award. Copy and cut out the one shown here. Pin the award to the child's clothes.

I can read
<u>My Aa Book</u>.
Just ask me!

_____
(name)

<u>CONCLUSION OF LESSON</u>

Remind the child to leave the award on until a grown-up at home asks him/her to read the book.

LETTER Bb

Bb

LESSON 1

Objective:

Child will

- visually recognize letter by name.
- recognize the sound /b/ in the initial position by naming words with b in that position.

Materials:

- Large chart with poem, *The Bumblebee* (see directions on p. x)
- Alphabet card with the letter Bb
- Letter Bb can, containing such items as:
  – miniature toy bear
  – picture of a bumblebee
  – plastic banana
  – bandage
  – bandana

Procedure:

STEP 1

1. Introduce the lesson with the poem, *The Bumblebee.*
2. Display the poem on an easel. You read the poem modeling 1-1 match with a pointer.

The Bumblebee

"Buzz, buzz, buzz,"
said the Bumblebee.
Here he comes, he's after me!
Oh no he's not, for I can see,
He's on his way to the apple tree!

3. Ask the whole group, "What letter of the alphabet do you think we are studying now?"
4. Ask children to echo read the poem several times.
5. Ask children for suggestions of movements for acting out the poem.
6. Reread the poem together, acting it out!
7. Put the poem aside.

STEP 2

1. Display the alphabet card with the letter Bb.
2. Ask children to name the letter they see on the alphabet card.
3. Hold up the letter Bb can.
4. Ask children to predict what would make sense in a Bb can.
5. Take each object/picture out of the can. Name them.
6. Ask children to repeat the name of each object/picture after you name it.
7. Show children a sample of the art activity.
8. You now do the art activity with the children, either as a small group or whole class.

ART ACTIVITY

Handprint Bumblebees

Materials:

▪ Blackline master of poem *The Bumblebee*
▪ Black construction paper 6″ × 9″
▪ Yellow construction paper 6″ × 9″
▪ Black and yellow paints
▪ Paintbrush
▪ Wiggly eyes
▪ Pompons
▪ Scissors
▪ Glue
▪ Stapler

Preparation:

Reproduce the poem *The Bumblebee* and staple it to the blackline of poem to the right side of the black construction paper.

Procedure:

1. You paint the child's palm, ring, and middle fingers with black paint. Press the child's hand down on the yellow paper.
2. Release hand and let paint dry.
3. You cut the handprint out. If time allows, child cuts out the handprint making sure to include "wings" on each side of the palm print.
4. Child paints yellow stripes on the body of the bee.
5. Child glues wiggly eyes on the face and pompons on the antennas.
6. Glue the bumblebee to the black construction paper.
7. Send the poem and art activity home. This gives family members an opportunity to reread the poem with the child, reinforcing the letter Bb.

CONCLUSION OF LESSON

Remind children they have learned to recognize letter Bb and they can think of words that have Bb in the initial position.

The Bumblebee

"Buzz, buzz, buzz," said the
bumblebee.

Here he comes, he's after me!

Oh no he's not, for I can see,

He's on his way to the apple
tree!

The Bumblebee

"Buzz, buzz, buzz," said the
bumblebee.

Here he comes, he's after me!

Oh no he's not, for I can see,

He's on his way to the apple
tree!

BLACKLINE MASTER—POEM

22

LESSON 2

Objective:

Children will read *My Bb Book* using 1-1 match.

Materials:

- Big Book—*My Bb Book* (see directions p. xi)
- Large poem—*The Bumblebee* (see directions p. x)
- Little books—*My Bb Book* (see directions p. xi)
- Crayons

Procedure:

1. Introduce the lesson with the poem *The Bumblebee.*
2. You reread the poem *The Bumblebee* modeling 1-1 match with a pointer. Children echo read the poem and act it out.
3. You hold up the "big book," *My Bb Book.* You read the title. Children echo read.
4. You go through each page of the "big book," covering all print. You name the picture on the page. Tell the children to listen for Bb words.
5. You read through the "big book" one time, modeling 1-1 match and directionality.
6. Invite the children to now read the "big book" with you. Model 1-1 match and directionality while reading.
7. The children read through the book a third time while you point to the words.

INDEPENDENT ACTIVITY

1. Reproduce blackline master of the little *My Bb Book.* Give children their own little *My Bb Book* and have them color it in.
2. After children color in their own little *My Bb Book,* they read their book to a partner.
3. You monitor the activity, looking for 1-1 match and directionality.
4. Collect the books.

CONCLUSION OF LESSON

1. You gather the whole group back together for whole group instruction.
2. Everyone rereads the "big book," *My Bb Book,* together.
3. While the children are reading the "big book," you model 1-1 match and directionality, while pointing to the words.

My Bb Book

_____
(name)

See the bee. Buzz!

See the boat.

- -

See the bird.

See the bus.

- -

See the balloon.

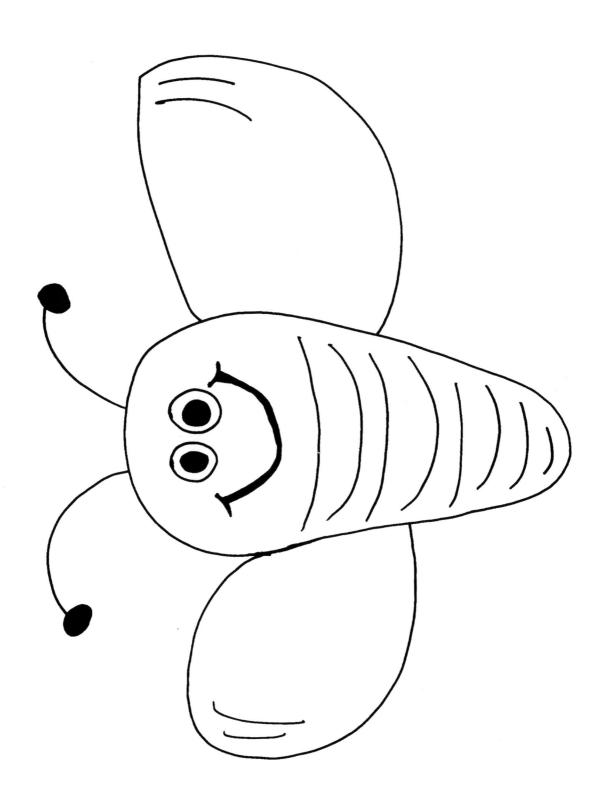

F

LESSON 3

Objective:

Child will focus on the 4 main cueing systems while reading little book, *My Bb Book.*

Materials:

- Big Book—*My Bb Book*
- Little books—*My Bb Book*
- Awards (see directions p. xii)
- Safety pins

Procedure:

1. Introduce the lesson with the "big book," *My Bb Book.*
2. You read the "big book" with the children, modeling 1-1 match and directionality while pointing to the words.
3. Echo read the book.

INDIVIDUALIZED INSTRUCTION

Note—The objective is to focus the child on the 4 main cueing systems:

- Meaning
- Visual
- Structure
- 1-1 Match

(See page viii for definition and more information.)

1. You now take each child, one at a time, having him/her read the little book, *My Bb Book,* to you. Child points to words while reading.
2. As the child is reading to you, you are listening for misread text and prompting the child with the appropriate question to help him/her correct the error. Your phrasing of the questions must be consistent with those in the "Examples of Misread Text."
3. Through repeated use of these techniques, the children will begin to ask themselves these questions. This indicates the child is now monitoring his/her own reading and is on the way to becoming an independent reader.
4. Following are specific examples of misread text by a child using little *My Bb Book.* Find the type of example that matches what your student has

read. After using the appropriate strategy questions and the child still can not recall the word, then tell the child the word! Teach the child right from the start that reading is *not* a trick!

5. The child's response may not be an exact match to the example. However, if the response is a similar mistake, prompt the child with the appropriate question.

Examples of Misread Text

Following are specific examples of misread text by a child using little *My Bb Book*. Find the type of example that matches what your student has read. Keep in mind that the child's response may not be an exact match to the example. However, if the response is a similar mistake, prompt the child with the appropriate question.

WHEN TO USE MEANING QUESTIONS

Objective:

Child must determine if what he/she has read makes sense in relation to the picture and in the context of the book he/she is reading.

Example

Child reads:	See the ship.
Text reads:	See the boat.

Strategy

Teacher:	"Does the ship make sense in a Bb Book?"
Child:	"No."
Teacher:	"What else could you try?"
Child:	"Boat."
Teacher:	"Good! Boat begins with b. *Good readers reread."*

WHEN TO USE STRUCTURE QUESTIONS

Objective:

Child must be able to hear what he/she has read and determine if it sounds right grammatically.

Example

Child reads: See to balloon.
Text reads: See the balloon.

Strategy

Teacher: "Does that sound right? Is that how people talk?"
"Child: "No."
Teacher: "What would sound right?"
Child: "See the balloon."
Teacher: "Good! *Good readers reread.*"

If the child hesitates and cannot recall the word, give it! Then have the child reread.

WHEN TO USE VISUAL QUESTIONS

Objective:

Child will use letter in the initial position to read a word in context.

Example

Child reads: See the robin.
Text reads: See the bird.

Strategy

You point to misread word: "What sound does the letter b make?"
Child: "Bbbbb."
Teacher: "Reread."
Child: "See the bird."

If the child hesitates and cannot recall the word, give it! Then have the child reread.

WHEN TO USE 1-1 QUESTIONS

Objective:

Child must understand what he/she says has to match the number of words on the page.

Example 1

Child reads: See the school bus.
Text reads: See the bus.

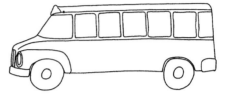

Strategy

Teacher: "Did your finger match the words?"

Child: "No."

Teacher: "Reread."

If the finger does not match the second time, you take the child's finger and point to the words together.

Example 2

Child reads: See bus.
Text reads: See the bus.

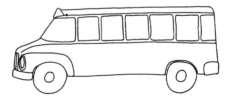

Strategy

Teacher: "Did your finger match the words?"

Child: "No."

Teacher: "Reread."

If the child responds, "Yes, my finger did match," take the child's finger and point to the words together.

LETTER Bb AWARD

When the child has successfully read his/her own My Bb Book to you, reward the child with an award. Copy and cut out the one shown here. Pin the award to the child's clothes.

I can read
My Bb Book.
Just ask me!

_____
(name)

CONCLUSION OF LESSON

Remind the child to leave the award on until a grown-up at home asks him/her to read the book.

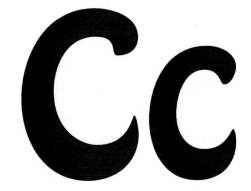

LETTER

Cc

LESSON 1

Objective:

Child will

∎ visually recognize letter by name.

∎ recognize the sound /c/ in the initial position by naming words with c in that position.

Materials:

∎ Large chart with poem, *The Caterpillar* (see directions on p. x)

∎ Any alphabet card with the letter Cc

∎ Letter Cc can, containing such items as:
  – plastic carrots, cookies, and cup
  – matchbox car

Procedure:

STEP 1

1. Introduce the lesson with the poem, *The Caterpillar.*
2. Display the poem on an easel. You read the poem modeling 1-1 match with a pointer.
3. Ask the whole group, "What letter of the alphabet do you think we are studying now?"

The Caterpillar

He creeps along the branch,
He climbs atop the tree.
He crawls around the leaf,
And all over me!

4. Ask children to echo read the poem several times.
5. Ask children for suggestions of movements for acting out the poem.
6. Reread the poem together, acting it out!
7. Put the poem aside.

STEP 2

1. Display the alphabet card with the letter Cc.
2. Ask children to name the letter they see on the alphabet card.
3. Hold up the letter Cc can.
4. Ask children to predict what would make sense in a Cc can.
5. Take each object/picture out of the can. Name them.
6. Ask children to repeat the name of each object/picture after you name it.
7. Show children a sample of the art activity.
8. You now do the art activity with the children. You decide whether to do the activity as a whole group or small group.

ART ACTIVITY

Creepy Caterpillars

Materials:

- Blackline master of poem *The Caterpillar*
- Crayons—brown and red
- Yellow construction paper 12" × 18"
- White construction paper 8-1/2" × 11"
- 6 - 2" in diameter green construction paper circles for each child
- Wiggly eyes
- 2 - 3" long pipe cleaners (any color), per child
- Stapler, glue, and Scotch tape

Preparation:

Reproduce the poem *The Caterpillar* and staple it to the right side of the yellow construction paper. Using 1 green circle per child, you poke the 2 pipe cleaners through the top of the circle. Turn over circle and Scotch tape the ends down. Bend the tops of the pipe cleaners slightly to make antennas.

Procedure:

1. Placing white paper lengthwise, children draw a branch horizontally across the white paper.
2. With teacher guidance, child glues 5 green circles along the branch. Circles should slightly overlap.
3. Using a red crayon, child draws a smile on the green circle that has the antennas.
4. With teacher guidance, child glues head on branch and wiggly eyes. Staple caterpillar to left side of the yellow construction paper.
5. Send the poem and art activity home. This gives family members an opportunity to reread the poem with the child, reinforcing the letter Cc.

CONCLUSION OF LESSON

Remind children they have learned to recognize letter Cc and they can think of words that have Cc in the initial position.

The Caterpillar

He creeps along the branch,

He climbs atop the tree.

He crawls around the leaf,

And all over me!

- -

The Caterpillar

He creeps along the branch,

He climbs atop the tree.

He crawls around the leaf,

And all over me!

LESSON 2

Objective:

Children will read *My Cc Book* using 1-1 match.

Materials:

- Big Book—*My Cc Book* (see directions p. xi)
- Large poem—*The Caterpillar* (see directions p. x)
- Little books—*My Cc Book* (see directions p. xi)
- Crayons

Procedure:

1. Introduce the lesson with the poem *The Caterpillar.*
2. You reread the poem *The Caterpillar* modeling 1-1 match with a pointer. Children echo read the poem and act it out.
3. You hold up the "big book," *My Cc Book.* You read the title. Children echo read.
4. You go through each page of the "big book," covering all print. You name the picture on the page. Tell the children to listen for Cc words.
5. You read through the "big book" one time, modeling 1-1 match and directionality.
6. Invite the children to now read the "big book" with you. Model 1-1 match and directionality while reading.
7. The children read through the book a third time while you point to the words.

INDEPENDENT ACTIVITY

1. Reproduce blackline master of the little *My Cc Book.* Give children their own little *My Cc Book* and have them color it in.
2. After children color in their own little *My Cc Book,* they read their book to a partner.
3. You monitor the activity, looking for 1-1 match and directionality.
4. Collect the books.

CONCLUSION OF LESSON

1. You gather the whole group back together for whole group instruction.
2. Everyone rereads the "big book," *My Cc Book,* together.
3. While the children are reading the "big book," you model 1-1 match and directionality, while pointing to the words.

My Cc Book

_____

(name)

- -

This is a cup.

This is a cat.

This is a cupcake. Yum! Yum!

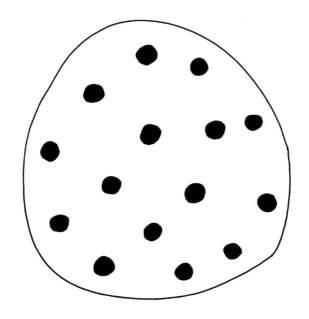

This is a cookie.

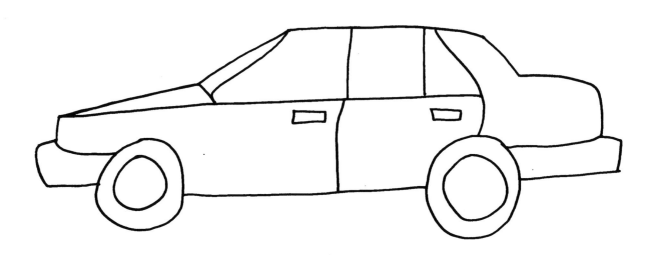

This is a car.

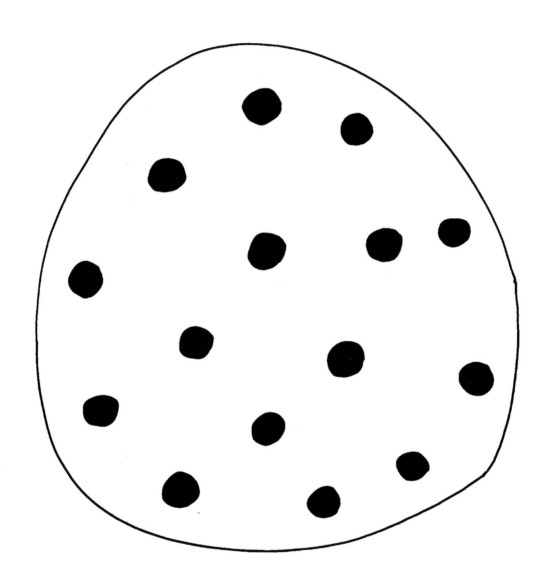

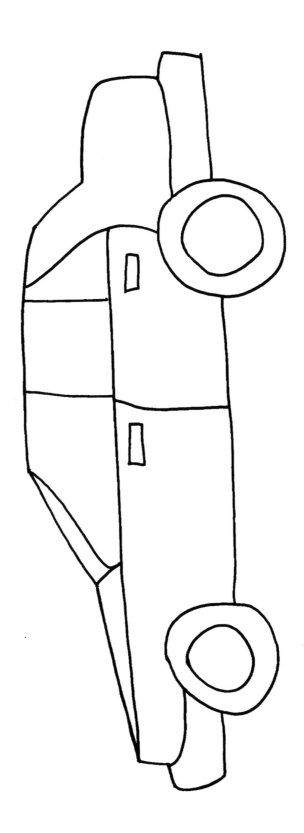

LESSON 3

Objective:

Child will focus on the 4 main cueing systems while reading little book, *My Cc Book.*

Materials:

- Big Book—*My Cc Book*
- Little books—*My Cc Book*
- Awards (see directions p. xii)
- Safety pins

Procedure:

1. Introduce the lesson with the "big book," *My Cc Book.*
2. You read the "big book" with the children, modeling 1-1 match and directionality while pointing to the words.
3. Echo read the book.

INDIVIDUALIZED INSTRUCTION

Note—The objective is to focus the child on the 4 main cueing systems:

- Meaning
- Visual
- Structure
- 1-1 Match

(See page viii for definition and more information.)

1. You now take each child, one at a time, having him/her read the little book, *My Cc Book,* to you. Child points to words while reading.
2. As the child is reading to you, you are listening for misread text and prompting the child with the appropriate question to help him/her correct the error. Your phrasing of the questions must be consistent with those in the "Examples of Misread Text."
3. Through repeated use of these techniques, the children will begin to ask themselves these questions. This indicates the child is now monitoring his/her own reading and is on the way to becoming an independent reader.
4. Following are specific examples of misread text by a child using little *My Cc Book.* Find the type of example that matches what your student has read. After using the appropriate strategy questions and the child still can

not recall the word, then tell the child the word! Teach the child right from the start that reading is *not* a trick!

5. The child's response may not be an exact match to the example. However, if the response is a similar mistake, prompt the child with the appropriate question.

Examples of Misread Text

Following are specific examples of misread text by a child using little *My Cc Book*. Find the type of example that matches what your student has read. Keep in mind that the child's response may not be an exact match to the example. However, if the response is a similar mistake, prompt the child with the appropriate question.

WHEN TO USE MEANING QUESTIONS

Objective:

Child must determine if what he/she has read makes sense in relation to the picture and in the context of the book he/she is reading.

Example

Child reads: This is a truck.
Text reads: This is a car.

Strategy

Teacher: "Look at the picture. Is that a truck?"

Child: "No. It's a car."

Teacher: "Good! *Good readers reread."*

WHEN TO USE STRUCTURE QUESTIONS

Objective:

Child must be able to hear what he/she has read and determine if it sounds right grammatically.

Example

Child reads: This a cat.
Text reads: This is a cat.

Strategy

Teacher:	"Does that sound right? Is that how people talk?"
Child:	"No."
Teacher:	"What would sound right?"
Child:	"This is a cat."
Teacher:	"Good! *Good readers reread."*

WHEN TO USE VISUAL QUESTIONS

Objective:

Child will use letter in the initial position to read a word in context.

Example

Child reads:	This is a glass.
Text reads:	This is a cup.

Strategy

You point to misread word: "What sound does the letter c make?"

Child:	"Ccc."
Teacher:	"Reread."
Child:	"This is a cup."

If the child hesitates and can not recall the word, give it! Then have the child reread.

WHEN TO USE 1-1 QUESTIONS

Objective:

Child must understand what he/she says has to match the number of words on the page.

Example 1

Child reads:	This is a chocolate chip cookie.
Text reads:	This is a cookie.

Strategy

Teacher: "Did your finger match the words?"

Child: "No."

Teacher: "Reread."

If the finger does not match the second time, you take the child's finger and point to the words together.

Example 2

Child reads: A cupcake.

Text reads: This is a cupcake. Yum Yum!

Strategy:

Teacher: "Did your finger match the words?"

Child: "No."

Teacher: "Reread."

If the child responds, "Yes, my finger did match," take the child's finger and point to the words together.

LETTER Cc AWARD

When the child has successfully read his/her own My Cc Book to you, reward the child with an award. Copy and cut out the one shown here. Pin the award to the child's clothes.

I can read
My Cc Book.
Just ask me!

_____
(name)

<u>CONCLUSION OF LESSON</u>

Remind the child to leave the award on until a grown-up at home asks him/her to read the book.

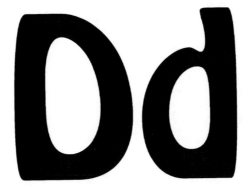

LESSON 1

Objective:

Child will:

■ visually recognize letter by name.

■ recognize the sound /d/ in the initial position by naming words with d in that position.

Materials:

■ Large chart with poem, *Dinosaurs* (see directions on p. x)

■ Any alphabet card with the letter Dd

■ Letter Dd can, containing such items as:

    – plastic dinosaur and dog

    – doll

    – dollar

    – doll's dress

Procedure:

STEP 1

1. Introduce the lesson with the poem, *Dinosaurs.*

2. Display the poem on an easel. You read the poem modeling 1-1 match with a pointer.

Dinosaurs

Dinosaurs lived long ago.
They were so big and strong, you
know!
Sharp teeth and claws,
Long tails, too.
Some that walked and some that
flew.
Though they don't live here
anymore,
We still adore the dinosaur!

3. Ask the whole group, "What letter of the alphabet do you think we are studying now?"
4. Ask children to echo read the poem several times.
5. Ask children for suggestions of movements for acting out the poem.
6. Reread the poem together, acting it out!
7. Put the poem aside.

STEP 2

1. Display the alphabet card with the letter Dd.
2. Ask children to name the letter they see on the alphabet card.
3. Hold up the letter Dd can.
4. Ask children to predict what would make sense in a Dd can.
5. Take each object/picture out of the can. Name them.
6. Ask children to repeat the name of each object/picture after you name it.
7. Show children a sample of the art activity.

8. You now do the art activity with the children, either as a small group or whole class.

ART ACTIVITY

Dan the Dinosaur

Materials:

- Blackline master of poem *Dinosaurs*
- Blackline master of dinosaur
- Purple construction paper 12″ × 18″
- Green watercolor paint
- Paint brushes
- Stapler
- 2-1/2″ long yellow construction paper triangles, per child
- Scissors

Preparation:

Reproduce the poem *Dinosaurs* and staple it to the right side of the purple construction paper.

Procedure:

1. Children paint the blackline master of the dinosaur with green water color paint.
2. Let dry.
3. With teacher guidance, children cut out dinosaur and glue on triangle teeth. Staple dinosaur to the left side of the poem.
4. Send the poem and art activity home. This gives family members an opportunity to reread the poem with the child, reinforcing the letter Dd.

CONCLUSION OF LESSON

Remind children they have learned to recognize letter Dd and they can think of words that have Dd in the initial position.

Dinosaurs

Dinosaurs lived long ago.

They were so big and strong,
you know! Sharp teeth and

claws, Long tails too.

Some that walked and some
that flew. Though they don't

live anymore, We still adore

the dinosaur!

- -

Dinosaurs

Dinosaurs lived long ago.

They were so big and strong,
you know! Sharp teeth and

claws, Long tails too.

Some that walked and some
that flew. Though they don't

live anymore, We still adore

the dinosaur!

BLACKLINE MASTER—POEM

BLACKLINE MASTER—DINOSAUR

LESSON 2

Objective:

Children will read *My Dd Book* using 1-1 match.

Materials:

- Big Book—*My Dd Book* (see directions p. xi)
- Large poem—*Dinosaurs* (see directions p. x)
- Little books—*My Dd Book* (see directions p. xi)
- Crayons

Procedure:

1. Introduce the lesson with the poem *Dinosaurs*.
2. You reread the poem *Dinosaurs* modeling 1-1 match with a pointer. Children echo read the poem and act it out.
3. You hold up the "big book," *My Dd Book*. You read the title. Children echo read.
4. You go through each page of the "big book," covering all print. You name the picture on the page. Tell the children to listen for Dd words.
5. You read through the "big book" one time, modeling 1-1 match and directionality.
6. Invite the children to now read the "big book" with you. Model 1-1 match and directionality while reading.
7. The children read through the book a third time while you point to the words.

INDEPENDENT ACTIVITY

1. Reproduce blackline master of the little *My Dd Book*. Give children their own little *My Dd Book* and have them color it in.
2. After children color in their own little *My Dd Book,* they read their book to a partner.
3. You monitor the activity, looking for 1-1 match and directionality.
4. Collect the books.

CONCLUSION OF LESSON

1. You gather the whole group back together for whole group instruction.
2. Everyone rereads the "big book," *My Dd Book,* together.
3. While the children are reading the "big book," you model 1-1 match and directionality, while pointing to the words.

My Dd Book

_____

(name)

A deer can run.

A dog can bark.

A duck can swim.

A door can open.

- -

A dinosaur can roar.
Can you?

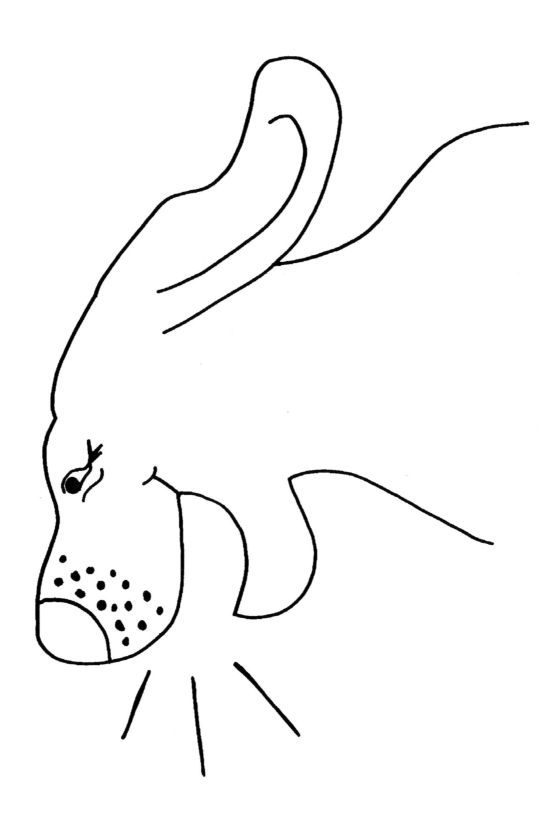

LESSON 3

Objective:

Child will focus on the 4 main cueing systems while reading little book, *My Dd Book.*

Materials:

- Big Book—*My Dd Book*
- Little books—*My Dd Book*
- Awards (see directions p. xii)
- Safety pins

Procedure:

1. Introduce the lesson with the "big book," *My Dd Book.*
2. You read the "big book" with the children, modeling 1-1 match and directionality while pointing to the words.
3. Echo read the book.

INDIVIDUALIZED INSTRUCTION

Note—The objective is to focus the child on the 4 main cueing systems:

- Meaning
- Visual
- Structure
- 1-1 Match

(See page viii for definition and more information.)

1. You now take each child, one at a time, having him/her read the little book, *My Dd Book,* to you. Child points to words while reading.
2. As the child is reading to you, you are listening for misread text and prompting the child with the appropriate question to help him/her correct the error. Your phrasing of the questions must be consistent with those in the "Examples of Misread Text."
3. Through repeated use of these techniques, the children will begin to ask themselves these questions. This indicates the child is now monitoring his/her own reading and is on the way to becoming an independent reader.
4. Following are specific examples of misread text by a child using little *My Dd Book.* Find the type of example that matches what your student has

read. After using the appropriate strategy questions and the child still can not recall the word, then tell the child the word! Teach the child right from the start that reading is *not* a trick!

5. The child's response may not be an exact match to the example. However, if the response is a similar mistake, prompt the child with the appropriate question.

Examples of Misread Text

Following are specific examples of misread text by a child using little *My Dd Book.* Find the type of example that matches what your student has read. Keep in mind that the child's response may not be an exact match to the example. However, if the response is a similar mistake, prompt the child with the appropriate question.

WHEN TO USE MEANING QUESTIONS

Objective:

Child must determine if what he/she has read makes sense in relation to the picture and in the context of the book he/she is reading.

Example

Child reads: A moose can run.
Text reads: A deer can run.

Strategy

Teacher: "Does moose make sense in a Dd book?"
Child: "No."
Teacher: "What else could you try?"
Child: "Deer."
Teacher: "Good! Deer begins with d. *Good readers reread.*"

WHEN TO USE STRUCTURE QUESTIONS

Objective:

Child must be able to hear what he/she has read and determine if it sounds right grammatically.

Example

Child reads: A dog is bark.
Text reads: A dog can bark.

Strategy

Teacher: "Does that sound right? Is that how people talk?"
Child: "No."
Teacher: "What would sound right?"
Child: "A dog can bark."
Teacher: "Good! *Good readers reread.*"

WHEN TO USE VISUAL QUESTIONS

Objective:

Child will use letter in the initial position to read a word in context.

Example

Child reads: A bird can swim.
Text reads: A duck can swim.

Strategy

You point to misread word: "What sound does the letter d make?"

Child: "Ddd."
Teacher: "Reread."
Child: "A duck can swim."

If the child hesitates and cannot recall the word, give it! Then have the child reread.

WHEN TO USE 1-1 QUESTIONS

Objective:

Child must understand what he/she says has to match the number of words on the page.

Example 1

Child reads: A dinosaur can roar. Can you roar?
Text reads: A dinosaur can roar. Can you?

Strategy

Teacher: "Did your finger match the words?"
Child: "No."
Teacher: "Reread."

If the finger does not match the second time, you take the child's finger and point to the words together.

Example 2

Child reads: A dinosaur roars. Can you?
Text reads: A dinosaur can roar. Can you?

Strategy

Teacher: "Did your finger match the words?"
Child: "No."
Teacher: "Reread."

If the child responds, "Yes, my finger did match," take the child's finger and point to the words together.

LETTER Dd AWARD

When the child has successfully read his/her My Dd Book to you, reward the child with an award. Copy and cut out the one shown here. Pin the award to the child's clothes.

I can read
<u>My Dd Book</u>.
Just ask me!

_____
(name)

<u>CONCLUSION OF LESSON</u>

Remind the child to leave the award on until a grown-up at home asks him/her to read the book.

LETTER

Ee

LESSON 1

Objective:

Child will

- visually recognize letter by name.
- be exposed to the various sounds /e/ makes in the initial position by naming words with e in that position.

Materials:

- Large chart with poem, *The Elephant* (see directions on p. x)
- Any alphabet card with the letter Ee
- Letter Ee can, containing such items as:
  - plastic egg
  - toy elephant
  - magazine picture of easel, eagle and eyes

Procedure:

STEP 1

1. Introduce the lesson with the poem, *The Elephant.*
2. Display the poem on an easel. You read the poem modeling 1-1 match with a pointer.

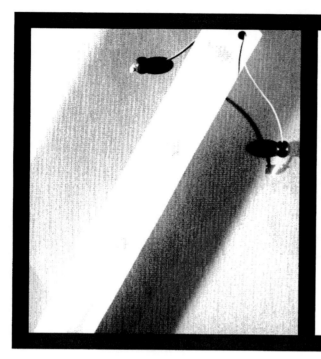

The Elephant

An elephant is a huge creature.
His long, long trunk is his best
feature. He uses it to help him
eat—peanuts, grass and hay.
It also helps him take a bath,
Quick—Get out of the way!

3. Ask the whole group, "What letter of the alphabet do you think we are studying now?"
4. Ask children to echo read the poem several times.
5. Ask children for suggestions of movements for acting out the poem.
6. Reread the poem together, acting it out!
7. Put the poem aside.

STEP 2

1. Display the alphabet card with the letter Ee.
2. Ask children to name the letter they see on the alphabet card.
3. Hold up the letter Ee can.
4. Ask children to predict what would make sense in an Ee can.
5. Take each object/picture out of the can. Name them.
6. Ask children to repeat the name of each object/picture after you name it.
7. Show children a sample of the art activity.
8. You now do the art activity with the children, either as a small group or whole class.

ART ACTIVITY

Elephants Trunk

Materials:

- Blackline master of poem *The Elephant*
- 1 - paper towel roll per child
- Red construction paper 6" × 9"
- Gray tempera paint
- Paint brushes
- Dish soap
- 2 - 1" diameter plastic beads with holes, per child
- Stapler
- Thin round elastic cut into 12" lengths, 1 per child, (elastic must be thin enough to fit through holes in the beads)
- Newspapers
- Hole punch
- Scissors

Preparation:

Reproduce the poem *The Elephant* and staple it to the right side of red construction paper. Thread piece of elastic through 1 of the beads. Tie knot at the end. At the end of the paper towel roll, punch 2 holes, across from each other. Mix 1/4 cup of dish soap into 3/4 cup of gray paint.

Procedure:

1. Children paint the paper towel roll.
2. Stand upright on newspaper to dry.
3. When dry, have each child hold his/her elephant trunk up to the nose, while you string elastic through the second hole in the paper towel roll.
4. String bead and tie a knot so it fits comfortably around the child's head.
5. Trim the end of the elastic.
6. Send the poem and art activity home. This gives family members an opportunity to reread the poem with the child, reinforcing the letter Ee.

CONCLUSION OF LESSON

Remind children they have learned to recognize letter Ee and they can think of words that have Ee in the initial position.

The Elephant

An elephant is a huge

creature. His long, long trunk

is his best feature.

He uses it to help him

eat—peanuts, grass and hay.

It also helps him take a bath,

Quick—Get out of the way!

The Elephant

An elephant is a huge

creature. His long, long trunk

is his best feature.

He uses it to help him

eat—peanuts, grass and hay.

It also helps him take a bath,

Quick—Get out of the way!

©1995 by Roberta Seckler Brown and Susan Carey

BLACKLINE MASTER—POEM

LESSON 2

Objective:

Children will read *My Ee Book* using 1-1 match.

Materials:

▌ Big Book—*My Ee Book* (see directions p. xi)
▌ Large poem—*The Elephant* (see directions p. x)
▌ Little books—*My Ee Book* (see directions p. xi)
▌ Crayons

Procedure:

1. Introduce the lesson with the poem *The Elephant.*
2. You reread the poem *The Elephant* modeling 1-1 match with a pointer. Children echo read the poem and act it out.
3. You hold up the "big book," *My Ee Book.* You read the title. Children echo read.
4. You go through each page of the "big book," covering all print. You name the picture on the page. Tell the children to listen for Ee words.
5. You read through the "big book" one time, modeling 1-1 match and directionality.
6. Invite the children to now read the "big book" with you. Model 1-1 match and directionality while reading.
7. The children read through the book a third time while you point to the words.

INDEPENDENT ACTIVITY

1. Reproduce blackline master of the little *My Ee Book.* Give children their own little *My Ee Book* and have them color it in.
2. After children color in their own little *My Ee Book,* they read their book to a partner.
3. You monitor the activity, looking for 1-1 match and directionality.
4. Collect the books.

CONCLUSION OF LESSON

1. You gather the whole group back together for whole group instruction.
2. Everyone rereads the "big book," *My Ee Book,* together.
3. While the children are reading the "big book," you model 1-1 match and directionality, while pointing to the words.

My Ee Book

_____

(name)

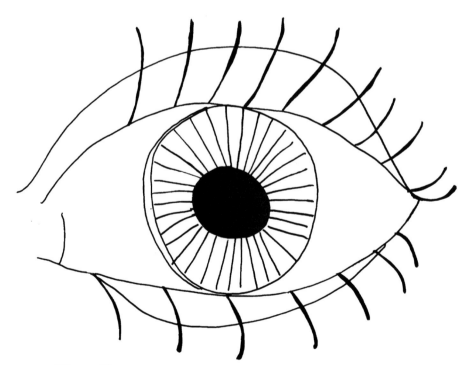

I have an eye.

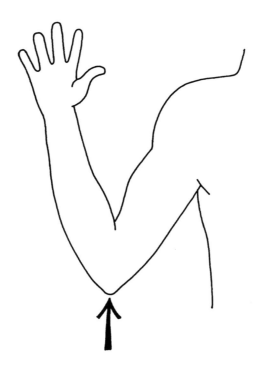

I have an elbow.

I have everything!

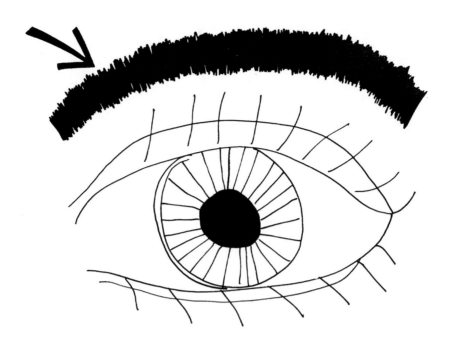

I have an eyebrow.

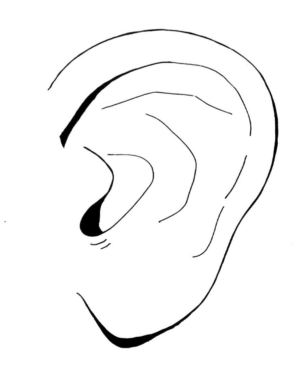

I have an ear.

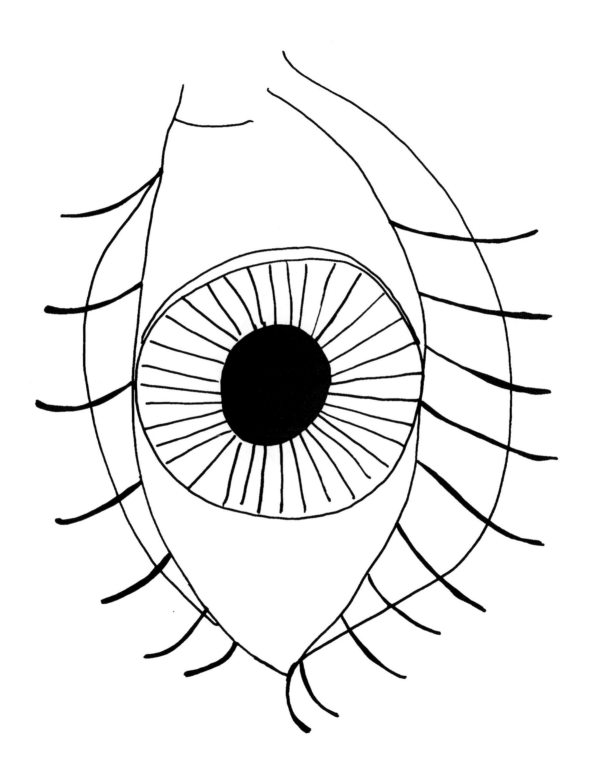

83

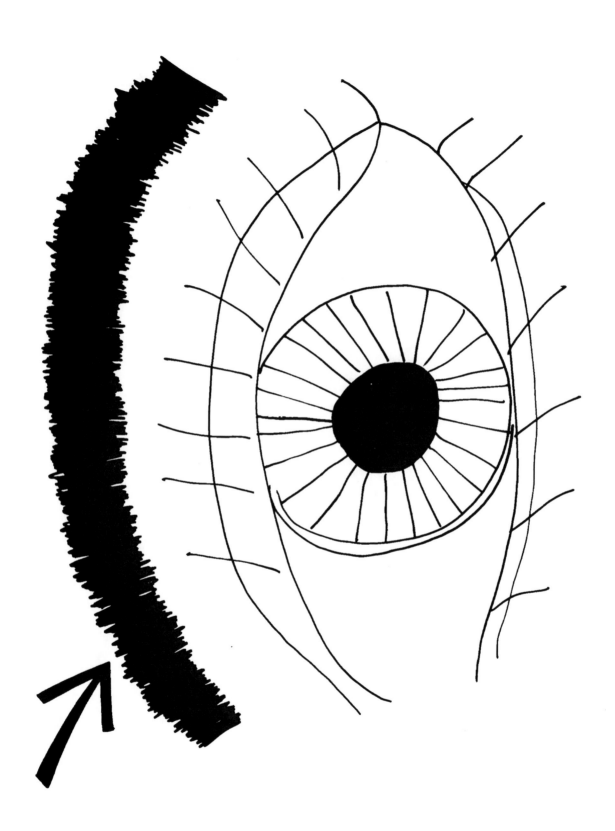

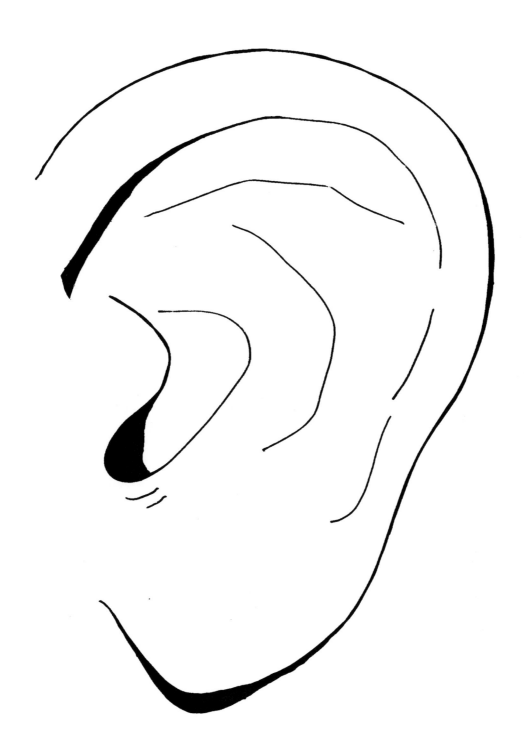

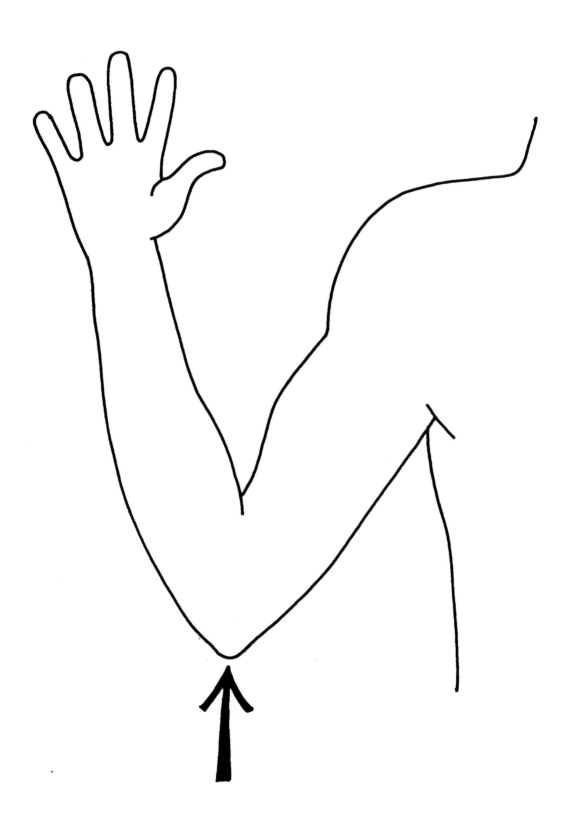

LESSON 3

Objective:

Child will focus on the 4 main cueing systems while reading little book, *My Ee Book.*

Materials:

▌ Big Book—*My Ee Book*
▌ Little books—*My Ee Book*
▌ Awards (see directions p. xii)
▌ Safety pins

Procedure:

1. Introduce the lesson with the "big book," *My Ee Book.*
2. You read the "big book" with the children, modeling 1-1 match and directionality while pointing to the words.
3. Echo read the book.

INDIVIDUALIZED INSTRUCTION

Note—The objective is to focus the child on the 4 main cueing systems:

▌ Meaning
▌ Visual
▌ Structure
▌ 1-1 Match

(See page viii for definition and more information.)

1. You now take each child, one at a time, having him/her read the little book, *My Ee Book,* to you. Child points to words while reading.
2. As the child is reading to you, you are listening for misread text and prompting the child with the appropriate question to help him/her correct the error. Your phrasing of the questions must be consistent with those in the "Examples of Misread Text."
3. Through repeated use of these techniques, the children will begin to ask themselves these questions. This indicates the child is now monitoring his/her own reading and is on the way to becoming an independent reader.
4. Following are specific examples of misread text by a child using little *My Ee Book.* Find the type of example that matches what your student has

read. After using the appropriate strategy questions and the child still cannot recall the word, then tell the child the word! Teach the child right from the start that reading is *not* a trick!

5. The child's response may not be an exact match to the example. However, if the response is a similar mistake, prompt the child with the appropriate question.

Examples of Misread Text

Following are specific examples of misread text by a child using little *My Ee Book.* Find the type of example that matches what your student has read. Keep in mind that the child's response may not be an exact match to the example. However, if the response is a similar mistake, prompt the child with the appropriate question.

WHEN TO USE MEANING QUESTIONS

Objective:

Child must determine if what he/she has read makes sense in relation to the picture and in the context of the book he/she is reading.

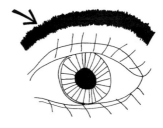

Example

Child reads: I have an eye.
Text reads: I have an eyebrow.

Strategy

Teacher:	"Look at the picture. Is the arrow pointing to the eye?"
Child:	"No."
Teacher:	"What else could you try?"
Child:	"I have an eyebrow."
Teacher:	"Good! *Good readers reread.*"

WHEN TO USE STRUCTURE QUESTIONS

Objective:

Child must be able to hear what he/she has read and determine if it sounds right grammatically.

Example

Child reads: I has an ear.
Text reads: I have an ear.

Strategy

Teacher:	"Does that sound right? Is that how people talk?"
Child:	"No."
Teacher:	"What would sound right?"
Child:	"I have an ear."
Teacher:	"Good! *Good readers reread.*"

WHEN TO USE VISUAL QUESTIONS

Objective:

Child will use letter in the initial position to read a word in context.

Example

Child reads: I have an arm.
Text reads: I have an elbow.

Strategy

You point to misread word: "What word do you know that starts with letter e and makes sense?"

Child:	"Elbow."
Teacher:	"Reread."
Child:	"I have an elbow."

If the child hesitates and cannot recall the word, give it! Then have the child reread.

WHEN TO USE 1-1 QUESTIONS

Objective:

Child must understand what he/she says has to match the number of words on the page.

Example 1

Child reads: I have all of them.
Text reads: I have everything!

Strategy

Teacher: "Did your finger match the words?"

Child: "No."

Teacher: "Reread."

If the finger does not match the second time, you take the child's finger and point to the words together.

Example 2

Child reads: I have eyes.
Text reads: I have an eye.

Strategy

Teacher: "Did your finger match the words?"

Child: "No."

Teacher: "Reread."

If the child responds, "Yes, my finger did match," take the child's finger and point to the words together.

LETTER Ee AWARD

When the child has successfully read his/her own My Ee Book to you, reward the child with an award. Copy and cut out the one shown here. Pin the award to the child's clothes.

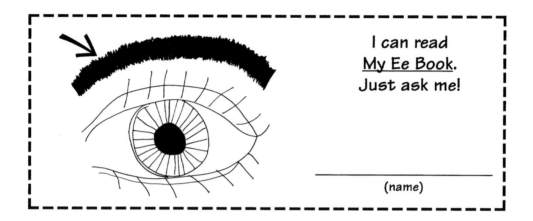

I can read
My Ee Book.
Just ask me!

_____
(name)

CONCLUSION OF LESSON

Remind the child to leave the award on until a grown-up at home asks him/her to read the book.

L E T T E R 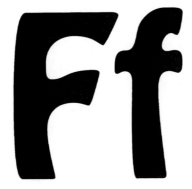

LESSON 1

Objective:

Child will

- visually recognize letter by name.
- recognize the sound /f/ in the initial position by naming words with f in that position.

Materials:

- Large chart with poem, *Funny Feet* (see directions on p. x)
- Any alphabet card with the letter Ff
- Letter Ff can, containing such items as:
  - plastic frog
  - magazine pictures of fish, fox, fork, feather

Procedure:

STEP 1

1. Introduce the lesson with the poem, *Funny Feet.*
2. Display the poem on an easel. You read the poem modeling 1-1 match with a pointer.

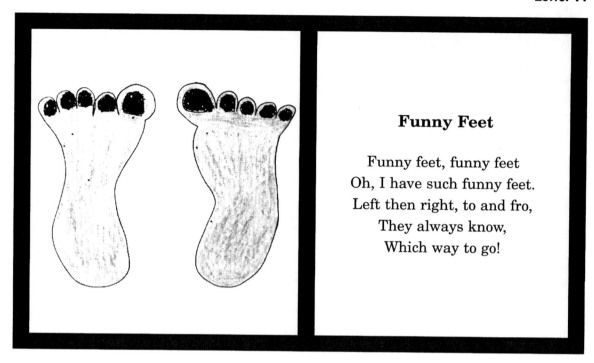

Funny Feet

Funny feet, funny feet
Oh, I have such funny feet.
Left then right, to and fro,
They always know,
Which way to go!

3. Ask the whole group, "What letter of the alphabet do you think we are studying now?"
4. Ask children to echo read the poem several times.
5. Ask children for suggestions of movements for acting out the poem.
6. Reread the poem together, acting it out!
7. Put the poem aside.

STEP 2

1. Display the alphabet card with the letter Ff.
2. Ask children to name the letter they see on the alphabet card.
3. Hold up the letter Ff can.
4. Ask children to predict what would make sense in an Ff can.
5. Take each object/picture out of the can. Name them.
6. Ask children to repeat the name of each object/picture after you name it.

7. Show children a sample of the art activity.
8. You now do the art activity with the children, either as a small group or whole class.

ART ACTIVITY

Funny Feet

Materials:

- Blackline master of poem *Funny Feet*
- Blackline master of funny feet
- Black construction paper 12″ × 18″
- Multicultural crayons
- Stapler
- Any color glitter

Preparation:

Reproduce the poem *Funny Feet* and staple it to the right side of the black construction paper.

Procedure:

1. Children color the blackline of funny feet using multicultural crayons.
2. With teacher guidance, children glue and glitter toe nails.
3. Let dry.
4. Staple funny feet to left side of the black construction paper.
5. Send the poem and art activity home. This gives family members an opportunity to reread the poem with the child, reinforcing the letter Ff.

CONCLUSION OF LESSON

Remind children they have learned to recognize letter Ff and they can think of words that have Ff in the initial position.

Funny Feet

Funny feet, funny feet

Oh, I have such funny feet.

Left then right,

To and fro,

They always know,

which way to go!

Funny Feet

Funny feet, funny feet

Oh, I have such funny feet.

Left then right,

To and fro,

They always know,

which way to go!

BLACKLINE MASTER—POEM

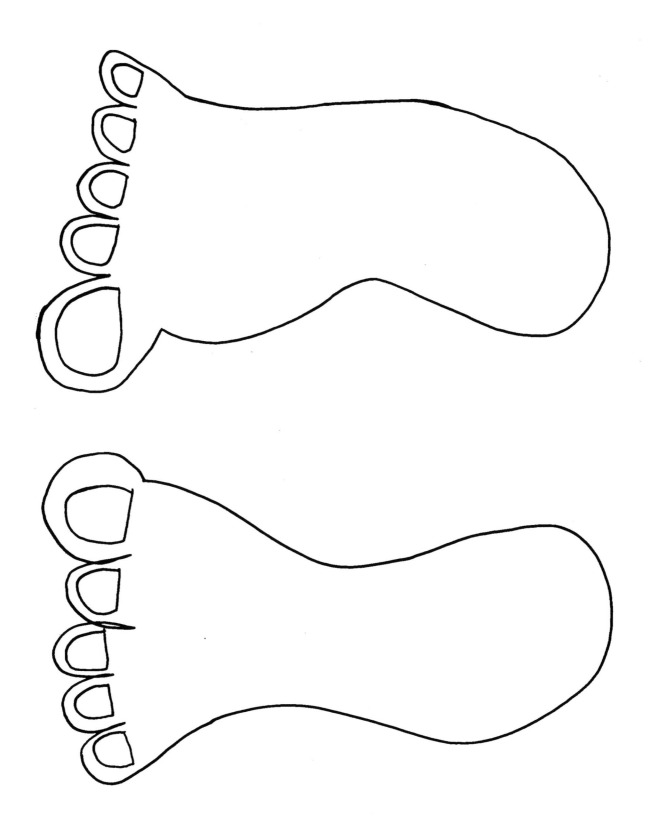

BLACKLINE MASTER—FUNNY FEET

LESSON 2

Objective:

Children will read *My Ff Book* using 1-1 match.

Materials:

■ Big Book—*My Ff Book* (see directions p. xi)
■ Large poem—*Funny Feet* (see directions p. x)
■ Little books—*My Ff Book* (see directions p. xi)
■ Crayons

Procedure:

1. Introduce the lesson with the poem *Funny Feet.*
2. You reread the poem *Funny Feet* modeling 1-1 match with a pointer. Children echo read the poem and act it out.
3. You hold up the "big book," *My Ff Book.* You read the title. Children echo read.
4. You go through each page of the "big book," covering all print. You name the picture on the page. Tell the children to listen for Ff words.
5. You read through the "big book" one time, modeling 1-1 match and directionality.
6. Invite the children to now read the "big book" with you. Model 1-1 match and directionality while reading.
7. The children read through the book a third time while you point to the words.

INDEPENDENT ACTIVITY

1. Reproduce blackline master of the little *My Ff Book.* Give children their own little *My Ff Book* and have them color it in.
2. After children color in their own little *My Ff Book,* they read their book to a partner.
3. You monitor the activity, looking for 1-1 match and directionality.
4. Collect the books.

CONCLUSION OF LESSON

1. You gather the whole group back together for whole group instruction.
2. Everyone rereads the "big book," *My Ff Book,* together.
3. While the children are reading the "big book," you model 1-1 match and directionality, while pointing to the words.

My Ff Book

_____

(name)

- -

A fox can run.

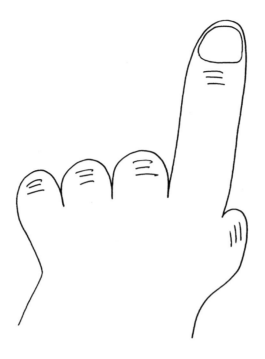

A finger can point.

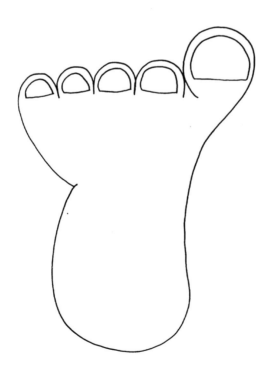

A foot can walk.

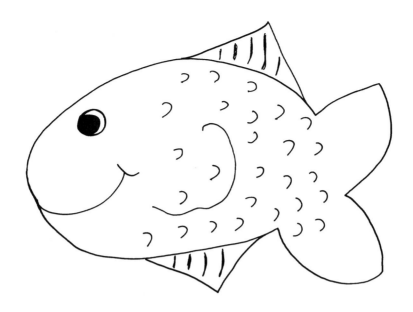

A fish can swim.

A frog can jump. So high!

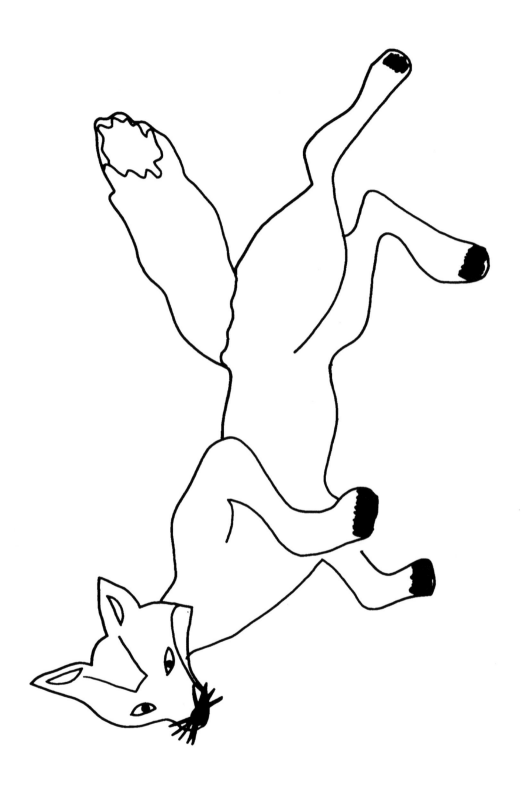

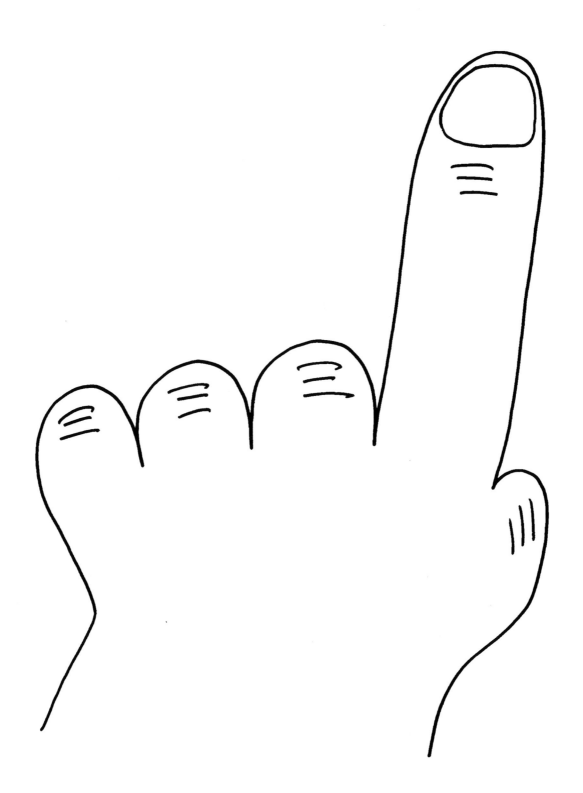

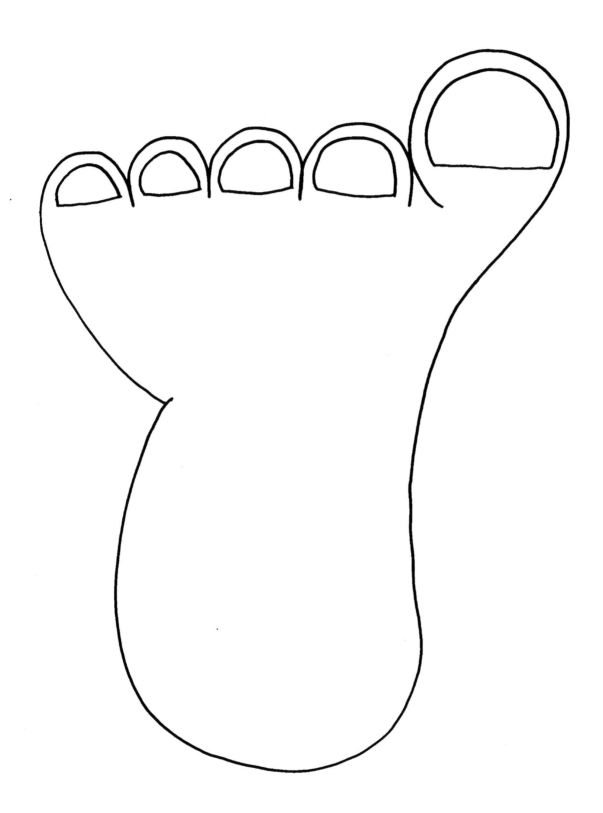

LESSON 3

Objective:

Child will focus on the 4 main cueing systems while reading little book, *My Ff Book.*

Materials:

▌ Big Book—*My Ff Book*
▌ Little books—*My Ff Book*
▌ Awards (see directions p. xii)
▌ Safety pins

Procedure:

1. Introduce the lesson with the "big book," *My Ff Book.*
2. You read the "big book" with the children, modeling 1-1 match and directionality while pointing to the words.
3. Echo read the book.

INDIVIDUALIZED INSTRUCTION

Note—The objective is to focus the child on the 4 main cueing systems:

▌ Meaning
▌ Visual
▌ Structure
▌ 1-1 Match

(See page viii for definition and more information.)

1. You now take each child, one at a time, having him/her read the little book, *My Ff Book,* to you. Child points to words while reading.
2. As the child is reading to you, you are listening for misread text and prompting the child with the appropriate question to help him/her correct the error. Your phrasing of the questions must be consistent with those in the "Examples of Misread Text."
3. Through repeated use of these techniques, the children will begin to ask themselves these questions. This indicates the child is now monitoring his/her own reading and is on the way to becoming an independent reader.
4. Following are specific examples of misread text by a child using little *My Ff Book.* Find the type of example that matches what your student has read. After using the appropriate strategy questions and the child still cannot recall the word, then tell the child the word! Teach the child right from the start that reading is *not* a trick!

5. The child's response may not be an exact match to the example. However, if the response is a similar mistake, prompt the child with the appropriate question.

Examples of Misread Text

Following are specific examples of misread text by a child using little *My Ff Book.* Find the type of example that matches what your student has read. Keep in mind that the child's response may not be an exact match to the example. However, if the response is a similar mistake, prompt the child with the appropriate question.

WHEN TO USE MEANING QUESTIONS

Objective:

Child must determine if what he/she has read makes sense in relation to the picture and in the context of the book he/she is reading.

Example

Child reads: A goldfish.
Text reads: A fish can swim.

Strategy

Teacher:	"Does goldfish make sense in an Ff book?"
Child:	"No."
Teacher:	"What else could you try?"
Child:	"Fish."
Teacher:	"Good! Fish begins with f. *Good readers reread.*"

WHEN TO USE STRUCTURE QUESTIONS

Objective:

Child must be able to hear what he/she has read and determine if it sounds right grammatically.

Example

Child reads: A feet can walk.
Text reads: A foot can walk.

Strategy

Teacher: "Does that sound right? Is that how people talk?"

Child: "No."

Teacher: "What would sound right?"

Child: "A foot can walk."

Teacher: "Good! *Good readers reread.*"

WHEN TO USE VISUAL QUESTIONS

Objective:

Child will use letter in the initial position to read a word in context.

Example

Child reads: A hand can point.
Text reads: A finger can point.

Strategy

You point to misread word: "What sound does the letter f make?"

Child: "Ffff."

Teacher: "Reread."

Child: "A finger can point."

If the child hesitates and cannot recall the word, give it! Then have the child reread.

WHEN TO USE 1-1 QUESTIONS

Objective:

Child must understand what he/she says has to match the number of words on the page.

Example 1

Child reads: A frog can jump high.
Text reads: A frog can jump. So high!

Strategy

Teacher: "Did your finger match the words?"

Child: "No."

Teacher: "Reread."

If the finger does not match the second time, you take the child's finger and point to the words together.

Example 2

Child reads: A fox can run fast.
Text reads: A fox can run.

Strategy

Teacher: "Did your finger match the words?"

Child: "No."

Teacher: "Reread."

If the child responds, "Yes, my finger did match," take the child's finger and point to the words together.

LETTER Ff AWARD

When the child has successfully read his/her own My Ff Book to you, reward the child with an award. Copy and cut out the one shown here. Pin the award to the child's clothes.

I can read
<u>My Ff Book</u>.
Just ask me!

_____
(name)

<u>CONCLUSION OF LESSON</u>

Remind the child to leave the award on until a grown-up at home asks him/her to read the book.

LESSON 1

Objective:

Child will

■ visually recognize letter by name.

■ recognize the sound /g/ in the initial position by naming words with a in that position.

Materials:

■ Large chart with poem, *My Guitar* (see directions on p. x)

■ Any alphabet card with the letter Gg

■ Letter Gg can, containing such items as:
  – plastic grapes
  – magazine pictures of girl, glass
  – stick of gum
  – toy gorilla

Procedure:

STEP 1

1. Introduce the lesson with the poem, *My Guitar.*

2. Display the poem on an easel. You read the poem modeling 1-1 match with a pointer.

My Guitar

On my guitar,
I can strum.
Play a note,
Sing and hum.
Hear the music,
Near and far.
As I strum,
On my guitar.

3. Ask the whole group, "What letter of the alphabet do you think we are studying now?"
4. Ask children to echo read the poem several times.
5. Ask children for suggestions of movements for acting out the poem.
6. Reread the poem together, acting it out!
7. Put the poem aside.

STEP 2

1. Display the alphabet card with the letter Gg.
2. Ask children to name the letter they see on the alphabet card.
3. Hold up the letter Gg can.
4. Ask children to predict what would make sense in a Gg can.
5. Take each object/picture out of the can. Name them.
6. Ask children to repeat the name of each object/picture after you name it.
7. Show children a sample of the art activity.
8. You now do the art activity with the children, either as a small group or whole class.

ART ACTIVITY

Groovy Guitar

Materials:

- Blackline master of poem *My Guitar*
- Blackline master of guitar
- Red construction paper 12″ × 18″
- Crayons
- Scissors
- 2-12″ length pieces of white yarn per child
- Hole punch
- Stapler
- Scotch tape

Preparation:

Reproduce the poem *My Guitar* and staple it to the right side of the red construction paper.

Punch 2 holes 1/2″ from the top of the guitar.

Punch 2 holes 1/2″ from the bottom of the guitar.

Try to align top and bottom holes.

Procedure:

1. Children color the blackline of guitar using crayons.
2. Children cut out guitar.
3. With teacher guidance, children string yarn through the holes.
4. Scotch tape yarn to the back of the guitar, so yarn does not fall through the holes.
5. Staple guitar to left side of the red construction paper.
6. Send the poem and art activity home. This gives family members an opportunity to reread the poem with the child, reinforcing the letter Gg.

CONCLUSION OF LESSON

Remind children they have learned to recognize letter Gg and they can think of words that have Gg in the initial position.

My Guitar

On my guitar I can strum,

Play a note, sing and hum.

Hear the music, near and far,

As I strum on my guitar.

My Guitar

On my guitar I can strum,

Play a note, sing and hum.

Hear the music, near and far,

As I strum on my guitar.

BLACKLINE MASTER—POEM

LESSON 2

Objective:

Children will read *My Gg Book* using 1-1 match.

Materials:

- Big Book—*My Gg Book* (see directions p. xi)
- Large poem—*My Guitar* (see directions p. x)
- Little books—*My Gg Book* (see directions p. xi)
- Crayons

Procedure:

1. Introduce the lesson with the poem *My Guitar.*
2. You reread the poem *My Guitar* modeling 1-1 match with a pointer. Children echo read the poem and act it out.
3. You hold up the "big book," *My Gg Book.* You read the title. Children echo read.
4. You go through each page of the "big book," covering all print. You name the picture on the page. Tell the children to listen for Gg words.
5. You read through the "big book" one time, modeling 1-1 match and directionality.
6. Invite the children to now read the "big book" with you. Model 1-1 match and directionality while reading.
7. The children read through the book a third time while you point to the words.

INDEPENDENT ACTIVITY

1. Reproduce blackline master of the little *My Gg Book.* Give children their own little *My Gg Book* and have them color it in.
2. After children color in their own little *My Gg Book,* they read their book to a partner.
3. You monitor the activity, looking for 1-1 match and directionality.
4. Collect the books.

CONCLUSION OF LESSON

1. You gather the whole group back together for whole group instruction.
2. Everyone rereads the "big book," *My Gg Book,* together.
3. While the children are reading the "big book," you model 1-1 match and directionality, while pointing to the words.

My Gg Book

_____

(name)

I see the goat.

I see the gate.

- -

I see the glasses.

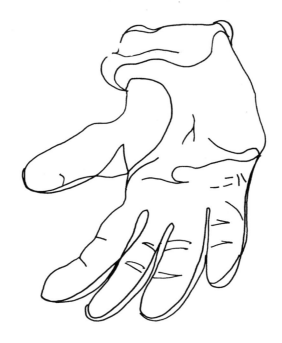

I see the glove.

I see the ghost. Boo!

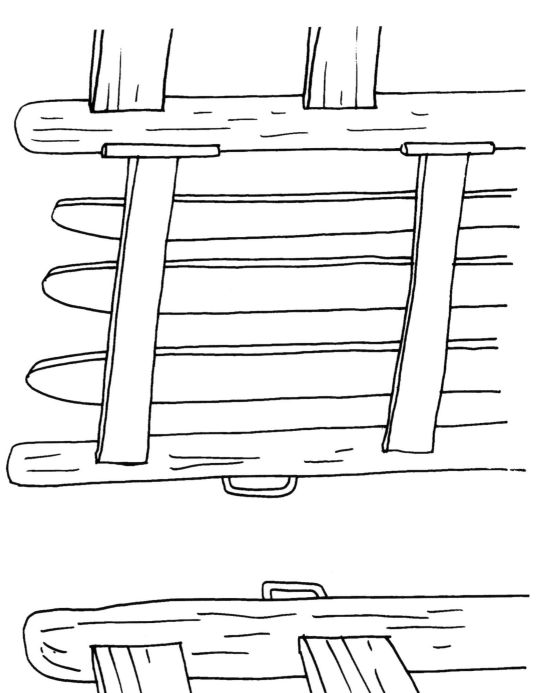

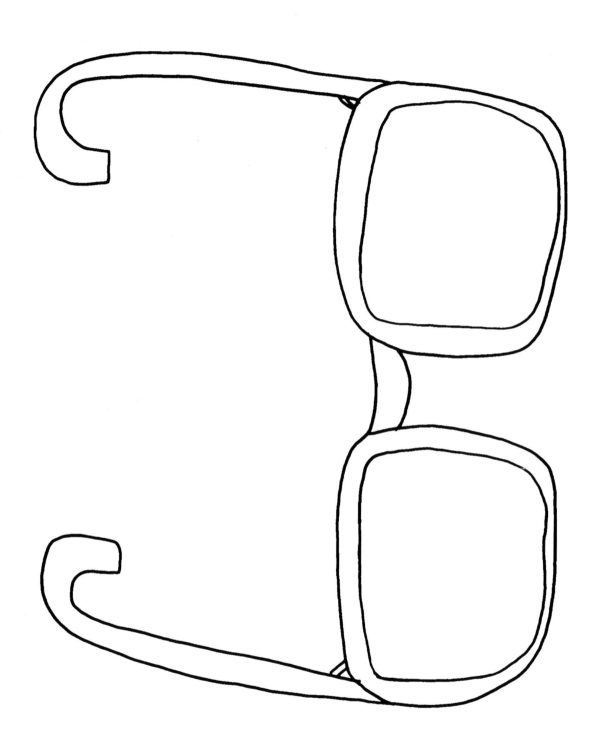

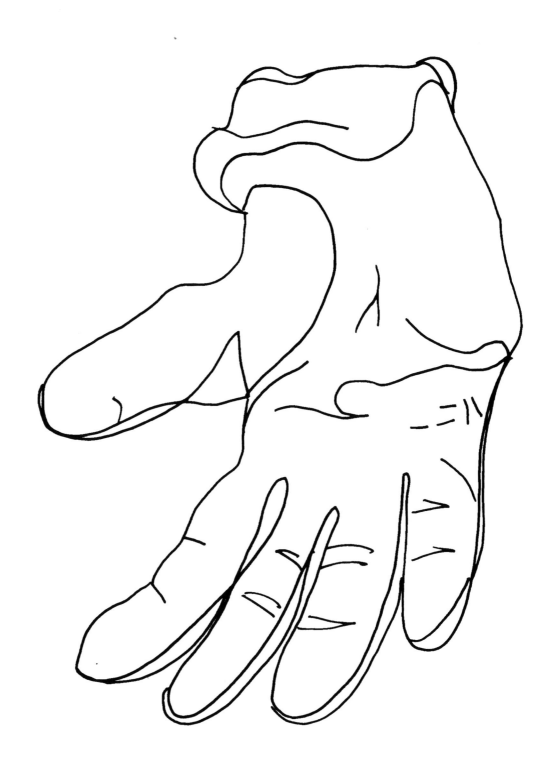

LESSON 3

Objective:

Child will focus on the 4 main cueing systems while reading little book, *My Gg Book.*

Materials:

- Big Book—*My Gg Book*
- Little books—*My Gg Book*
- Awards (see directions p. xii)
- Safety pins

Procedure:

1. Introduce the lesson with the "big book," *My Gg Book.*
2. You read the "big book" with the children, modeling 1-1 match and directionality while pointing to the words.
3. Echo read the book.

INDIVIDUALIZED INSTRUCTION

Note—The objective is to focus the child on the 4 main cueing systems:

- Meaning
- Visual
- Structure
- 1-1 Match

(See page viii for definition and more information.)

1. You now take each child, one at a time, having him/her read the little book, *My Gg Book,* to you. Child points to words while reading.
2. As the child is reading to you, you are listening for misread text and prompting the child with the appropriate question to help him/her correct the error. Your phrasing of the questions must be consistent with those in the "Examples of Misread Text."
3. Through repeated use of these techniques, the children will begin to ask themselves these questions. This indicates the child is now monitoring his/her own reading and is on the way to becoming an independent reader.
4. Following are specific examples of misread text by a child using little *My Gg Book.* Find the "type" of example that matches what your student has read. After using the appropriate strategy questions and the child still cannot recall the word, then tell the child the word! Teach the child right from the start that reading is *not* a trick!

5. The child's response may not be an exact match to the example. However, if the response is a similar mistake, prompt the child with the appropriate question.

Examples of Misread Text

Following are specific examples of misread text by a child using little *My Gg Book.* Find the type of example that matches what your student has read. Keep in mind that the child's response may not be an exact match to the example. However, if the response is a similar mistake, prompt the child with the appropriate question.

WHEN TO USE MEANING QUESTIONS

Objective:

Child must determine if what he/she has read makes sense in relation to the picture and in the context of the book he/she is reading.

Example

Child reads: I see the dog.
Text reads: I see the goat.

Strategy

Teacher: "Look at the picture. Is that a dog?"

Child: "No. It's a goat."

Teacher: "Good! *Good readers reread.*"

WHEN TO USE STRUCTURE QUESTIONS

Objective:

Child must be able to hear what he/she has read and determine if it sounds right grammatically.

Example

Child reads: I see gate.
Text reads: I see the gate.

Strategy

Teacher: "Does that sound right? Is that how people talk?"

Child: "No."

Teacher: "What would sound right?"

Child: "I see the gate."

Teacher: "Good! *Good readers reread.*"

WHEN TO USE VISUAL QUESTIONS

Objective:

Child will use letter in the initial position to read a word in context.

Example

Child reads: I see the fence.
Text reads: I see the gate.

Strategy

You point to misread word: "What sound does the letter g make?"

Child: "Gggg."

Teacher: "Reread."

Child: "I see the gate."

If the child hesitates and cannot recall the word, give it! Then have the child reread.

WHEN TO USE 1-1 QUESTIONS

Objective:

Child must understand what he/she says has to match the number of words on the page.

Example 1

Child reads: I see the ghost.
Text reads: I see the ghost. Boo!

Strategy

Teacher: "Did your finger match the words?"

Child: "No."

Teacher: "Reread."

If the finger does not match the second time, you take the child's finger and point to the words together.

Example 2

Child reads: I see the billy goat.
Text reads: I see the goat.

Strategy

Teacher: "Did your finger match the words?"

Child: "No."

Teacher: "Reread."

If the child responds, "Yes, my finger did match," take the child's finger and point to the words together.

LETTER Gg AWARD

When the child has successfully read his/her own My Gg Book to you, reward the child with an award. Copy and cut out the one shown here. Pin the award to the child's clothes.

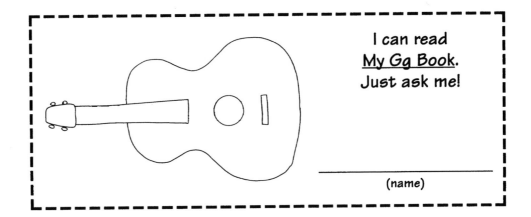

I can read
My Gg Book.
Just ask me!

_____
(name)

CONCLUSION OF LESSON

Remind the child to leave the award on until a grown-up at home asks him/her to read the book.

LETTER Hh

LESSON 1

Objective:

Child will

- visually recognize letter by name.
- recognize the sound /h/ in the initial position by naming words with h in that position.

Materials:

- Large chart with poem, *Hippos* (see directions on p. x)
- Any alphabet card with the letter Hh
- Letter Hh can, containing such items as:
    - plastic hot dog
    - red paper heart
    - toy hippopotamus, horse
    - photograph of a house

Procedure:

STEP 1

1. Introduce the lesson with the poem, *Hippos.*

Hippos

Hippos are huge!
They eat tons of grass.
What would we do,
if one came to our class?
Would we ask him to stay,
if he fit through the door,
Or send him away,
if he laid on the floor?
Hippos are huge!

2. Display the poem on an easel. You read the poem modeling 1-1 match with a pointer.

3. Ask the whole group, "What letter of the alphabet do you think we are studying now?"

4. Ask children to echo read the poem several times.

5. Ask children for suggestions of movements for acting out the poem.

6. Reread the poem together, acting it out!

7. Put the poem aside.

STEP 2

1. Display the alphabet card with the letter Hh.

2. Ask children to name the letter they see on the alphabet card.

3. Hold up the letter Hh can.

4. Ask children to predict what would make sense in an Hh can.

5. Take each object/picture out of the can. Name them.

6. Ask children to repeat the name of each object/picture after you name it.

7. Show children a sample of the art activity.

8. You now do the art activity with the children, either as a small group or whole class.

ART ACTIVITY

Huge Hippos

Materials:

- Blackline master of poem *Hippos*
- Blackline master of hippo
- Pink construction paper 12″ × 18″
- Brown construction paper 6″ × 9″ (1 per child)
- Green construction paper 3″ × 3″ (1 per child)
- Gray crayons
- Wiggly eyes
- Glue
- Scissors
- Stapler

Preparation:

Reproduce the poem *Hippos* and staple it to the right side of the pink construction paper.

Procedure:

1. Children color the blackline of the hippo using gray crayons.
2. Children cut out hippos.
3. With teacher guidance, children glue on wiggly eyes.
4. Let dry.
5. Children tear brown construction paper into small pieces.
6. Children overlap torn brown paper, when gluing to the 12″ × 18″ green construction paper next to the poem.
7. With teacher guidance, children glue the hippo on top of the torn brown paper.
8. With teacher guidance, children tear and glue small green paper near the hippo's mouth.
9. Send the poem and art activity home. This gives family members an opportunity to reread the poem with the child, reinforcing the letter Hh.

CONCLUSION OF LESSON

Remind children they have learned to recognize letter Hh and they can think of words that have Hh in the initial position.

Hippos

Hippos are huge!

They eat tons of grass.

What would we do if one came

    to our class?

Would we ask him to stay if

he fit through the door,

Or... send him away, if he laid

    on the floor?

Hippos are huge!

- -

Hippos

Hippos are huge!

They eat tons of grass.

What would we do if one came

    to our class?

Would we ask him to stay if

he fit through the door,

Or... send him away, if he laid

    on the floor?

Hippos are huge!

BLACKLINE MASTER—POEM

LESSON 2

Objective:

Children will read *My Hh Book* using 1-1 match.

Materials:

- Big Book—*My Hh Book* (see directions p. xi)
- Large poem—*Hippos* (see directions p. x)
- Little books—*My Hh Book* (see directions p. xi)
- Crayons

Procedure:

1. Introduce the lesson with the poem *Hippos.*
2. You reread the poem *Hippos* modeling 1-1 match with a pointer. Children echo read the poem and act it out.
3. You hold up the "big book," *My Hh Book.* You read the title. Children echo read.
4. You go through each page of the "big book," covering all print. You name the picture on the page. Tell the children to listen for Hh words.
5. You read through the "big book" one time, modeling 1-1 match and directionality.
6. Invite the children to now read the "big book" with you. Model 1-1 match and directionality while reading.
7. The children read through the book a third time while you point to the words.

INDEPENDENT ACTIVITY

1. Reproduce blackline master of the little *My Hh Book.* Give children their own little *My Hh Book* and have them color it in. On the last page of their book, have the children draw and color their house.
2. After children color in their own little *My Hh Book,* they read their book to a partner.
3. You monitor the activity, looking for 1-1 match and directionality.
4. Collect the books.

CONCLUSION OF LESSON

1. You gather the whole group back together for whole group instruction.
2. Everyone rereads the "big book," *My Hh Book,* together.
3. While the children are reading the "big book," you model 1-1 match and directionality, while pointing to the words.

My Hh Book

_____

(name)

- -

This is a heart.

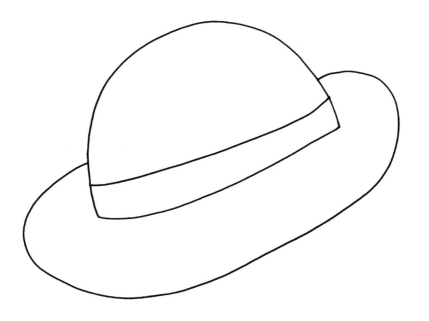

This is a hat.

- -

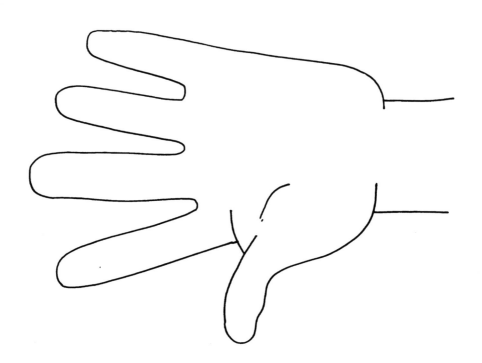

This is a hand.

This is a hen.

This is a house. Mine!

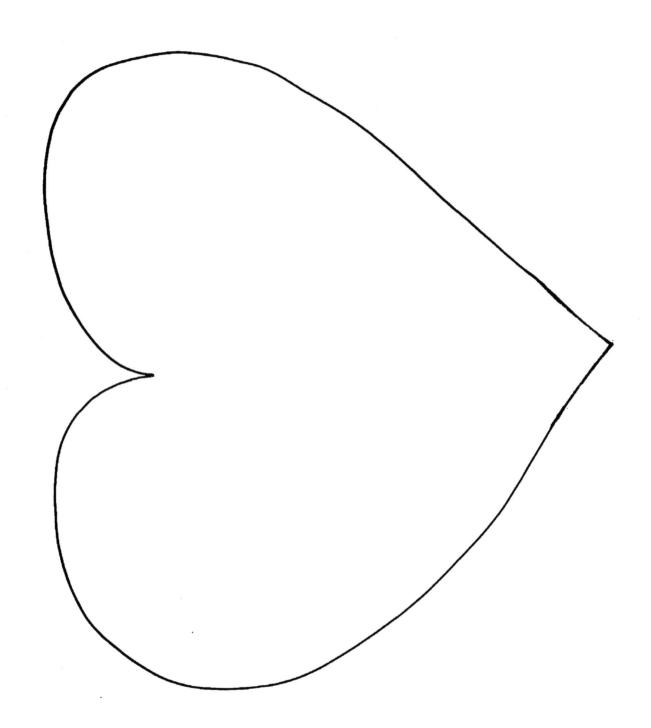

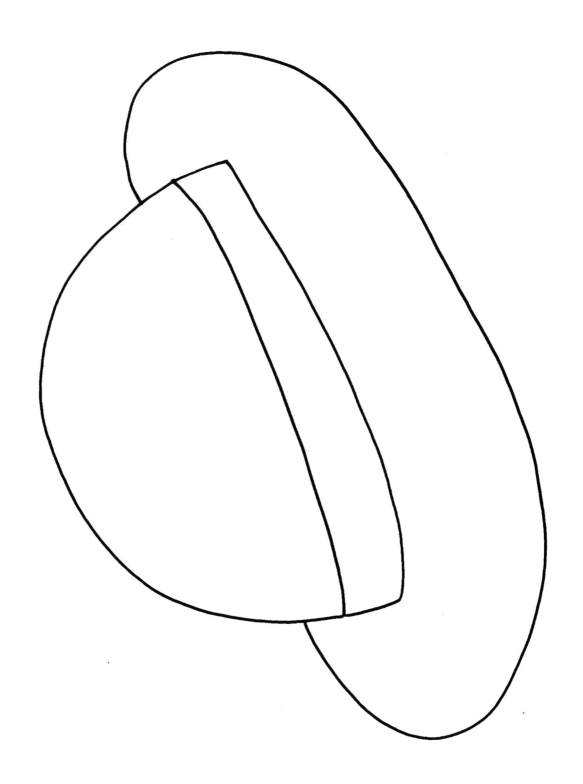

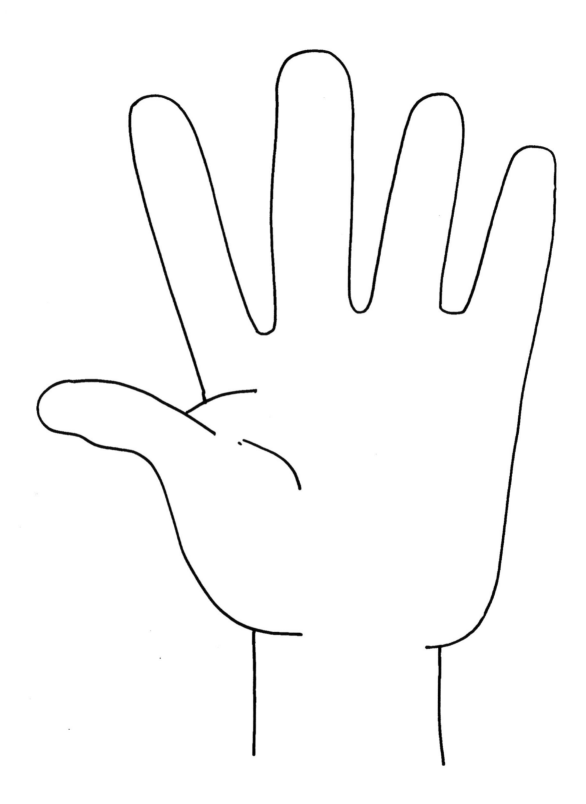

LESSON 3

Objective:

Child will focus on the 4 main cueing systems while reading little book, *My Hh Book.*

Materials:

- Big Book—*My Hh Book*
- Little books—*My Hh Book*
- Awards (see directions p. xii)
- Safety pins

Procedure:

1. Introduce the lesson with the "big book," *My Hh Book.*
2. You read the "big book" with the children, modeling 1-1 match and directionality while pointing to the words.
3. Echo read the book.

INDIVIDUALIZED INSTRUCTION

Note—The objective is to focus the child on the 4 main cueing systems:

- Meaning
- Visual
- Structure
- 1-1 Match

(See page viii for definition and more information.)

1. You now take each child, one at a time, having him/her read the little book, *My Hh Book,* to you. Child points to words while reading.
2. As the child is reading to you, you are listening for misread text and prompting the child with the appropriate question to help him/her correct the error. Your phrasing of the questions must be consistent with those in the "Examples of Misread Text."
3. Through repeated use of these techniques, the children will begin to ask themselves these questions. This indicates the child is now monitoring his/her own reading and is on the way to becoming an independent reader.
4. Following are specific examples of misread text by a child using little *My Hh Book.* Find the type of example that matches what your student has read. After using the appropriate strategy questions and the child still cannot recall the word, then tell the child the word! Teach the child right from the start that reading is *not* a trick!

5. The child's response may not be an exact match to the example. However, if the response is a similar mistake, prompt the child with the appropriate question.

Examples of Misread Text

Following are specific examples of misread text by a child using little *My Hh Book.* Find the type of example that matches what your student has read. Keep in mind that the child's response may not be an exact match to the example. However, if the response is a similar mistake, prompt the child with the appropriate question.

WHEN TO USE MEANING QUESTIONS

Objective:

Child must determine if what he/she has read makes sense in relation to the picture and in the context of the book he/she is reading.

Example

| Child reads: | This is a shape. |
| Text reads: | This is a heart. |

Strategy

Teacher:	"Does shape make sense in an Hh book?"
Child:	"No."
Teacher:	"What else could you try?"
Child:	"Heart."
Teacher:	"Good! Heart begins with h. *Good readers reread."*

WHEN TO USE STRUCTURE QUESTIONS

Objective:

Child must be able to hear what he/she has read and determine if it sounds right grammatically.

Example

Child reads: This a heart.
Text reads: This is a heart.

Strategy

Teacher: "Does that sound right? Is that how people talk?"
Child: "No."
Teacher: "What would sound right?"
Child: "This is a heart."
Teacher: "Good! *Good readers reread.*"

WHEN TO USE VISUAL QUESTIONS

Objective:
Child will use letter in the initial position to read a word in context.

Example

Child reads: This is a rooster.
Text reads: This is a hen.

Strategy

You point to misread word: "What sound does the letter h make?"

Child: "Hhhh."
Teacher: "Reread."
Child: "This is a hen."

If the child hesitates and cannot recall the word, give it! Then have the child reread.

WHEN TO USE 1-1 QUESTIONS

Objective:

Child must understand what he/she says has to match the number of words on the page.

Example 1

Child reads: This is my house.
Text reads: This is a house. Mine!

Strategy

Teacher: "Did your finger match the words?"

Child: "No."

Teacher: "Reread."

If the finger does not match the second time, you take the child's finger and point to the words together.

Example 2

Child reads: This is a big hand.
Text reads: This is a hand.

Strategy

Teacher: "Did your finger match the words?"

Child: "No."

Teacher: "Reread."

If the child responds, "Yes, my finger did match," take the child's finger and point to the words together.

LETTER Hh AWARD

When the child has successfully read his/her own My Hh Book to you, reward the child with an award. Copy and cut out the one shown here. Pin the award to the child's clothes.

I can read
<u>My Hh Book</u>.
Just ask me!

_____
(name)

CONCLUSION OF LESSON

Remind the child to leave the award on until a grown-up at home asks him/her to read the book.

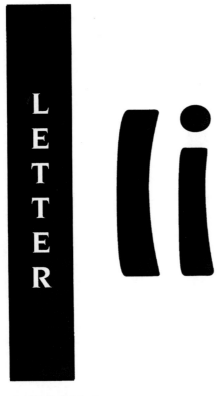

LETTER Ii

LESSON 1

Objective:

Child will

▪ visually recognize letter by name.
▪ recognize the sound /i/ in the initial position by naming words with i in that position.

Materials:

▪ Large chart with poem, *Ice Cream* (see directions on p. x)
▪ Any alphabet card with the letter Ii
▪ Letter Ii can, containing such items as:
  – ice cube tray
  – magazine picture of ice cream
  – mark off 1″ on a ruler

Procedure:

STEP 1

1. Introduce the lesson with the poem, *Ice Cream.*
2. Display the poem on an easel. You read the poem modeling 1-1 match with a pointer.

Ice Cream

I like ice cream. Yes I do!
One scoop for me?
No! Make that two!
Hmmm, two scoops of ice cream,
I want more.
How about three?
No, make that four!
Count 1
Count 2
Count 3
Count 4
Splat! "Oh no! It's on the floor!"

3. Ask the whole group, "What letter of the alphabet do you think we are studying now?"
4. Ask children to echo read the poem several times.
5. Ask children for suggestions of movements for acting out the poem.
6. Reread the poem together, acting it out!
7. Put the poem aside.

STEP 2

1. Display the alphabet card with the letter Ii.
2. Ask children to name the letter they see on the alphabet card.
3. Hold up the letter Ii can.
4. Ask children to predict what would make sense in an Ii can.
5. Take each object/picture out of the can. Name them.
6. Ask children to repeat the name of each object/picture after you name it.
7. Show children a sample of the art activity.

8. You now do the art activity with the children, either as a small group or whole class.

ART ACTIVITY

Ice Cream Cones

Materials:

- Blackline master of poem *Ice Cream*
- Blackline master of ice cream cone
- White construction paper 6″ × 9″
- Brown crayons
- Stapler
- Glue
- Water colors
- Brushes

Preparation:

Reproduce the poem *Ice Cream* and staple the poem to the right side of the white construction paper.

Procedure:

1. Children color the blackline of ice cream cone using brown crayons.
2. Children paint the scoops, each one a different color.
3. Let dry.
4. When dry, cut out scoops and cone.
5. With teacher guidance, children glue cone and scoops to white paper.
6. Send the poem and art activity home. This gives family members an opportunity to reread the poem with the child, reinforcing the letter Ii.

CONCLUSION OF LESSON

Remind children they have learned to recognize letter Ii and they can think of words that have Ii in the initial position.

Ice Cream

I like ice cream, Yes I do!

One scoop for me?

No! Make that two!

Hmmm, two scoops of ice cream,

I want more. How about three?

No, make that four!

Count 1, Count 2, Count 3,

Count 4. Splat!

"Oh no! It's on the floor!"

- -

Ice Cream

I like ice cream, Yes I do!

One scoop for me?

No! Make that two!

Hmmm, two scoops of ice cream,

I want more. How about three?

No, make that four!

Count 1, Count 2, Count 3,

Count 4. Splat!

"Oh no! It's on the floor!"

BLACKLINE MASTER—ICE CREAM CONE

155

LESSON 2

Objective:

Children will read *My Ii Book* using 1-1 match.

Materials:

- Big Book—*My Ii Book* (see directions p. xi)
- Large poem—*Ice Cream* (see directions p. x)
- Little books—*My Ii Book* (see directions p. xi)
- Crayons

Procedure:

1. Introduce the lesson with the poem *Ice Cream.*
2. You reread the poem *Ice Cream* modeling 1-1 match with a pointer. Children echo read the poem and act it out.
3. You hold up the "big book," *My Ii Book.* You read the title. Children echo read.
4. You go through each page of the "big book," covering all print. You name the picture on the page. Tell the children to listen for Ii words.
5. You read through the "big book" one time, modeling 1-1 match and directionality.
6. Invite the children to now read the "big book" with you. Model 1-1 match and directionality while reading.
7. The children read through the book a third time while you point to the words.

INDEPENDENT ACTIVITY

1. Reproduce blackline master of the little *My Ii Book.* Give children their own little *My Ii Book* and have them color it in.
2. After children color in their own little *My Ii Book,* they read their book to a partner.
3. You monitor the activity, looking for 1-1 match and directionality.
4. Collect the books.

CONCLUSION OF LESSON

1. You gather the whole group back together for whole group instruction.
2. Everyone rereads the "big book," *My Ii Book,* together.
3. While the children are reading the "big book," you model 1-1 match and directionality, while pointing to the words.

My Ii Book

_____
(name)

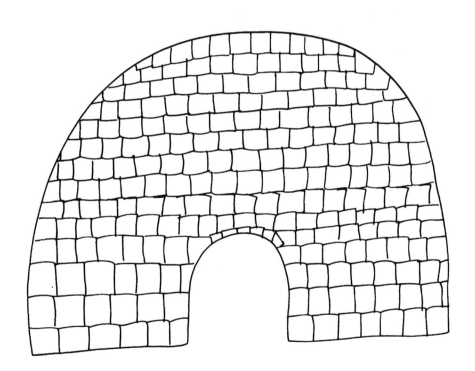

I see the igloo.

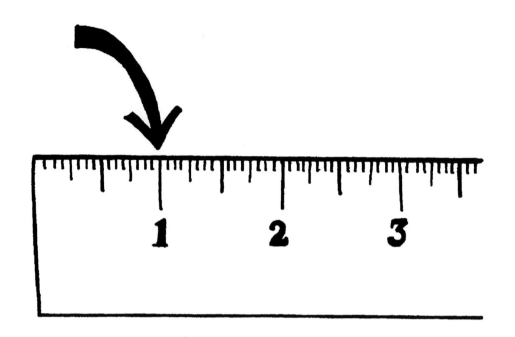

I see the inch.

- -

I see the island.

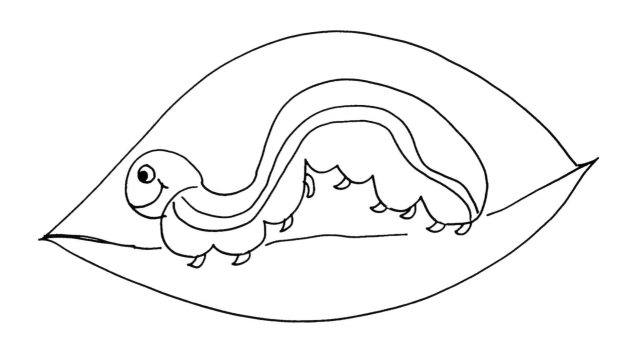

I see the inchworm.

- -

I see the ice cream.
Eat it up!

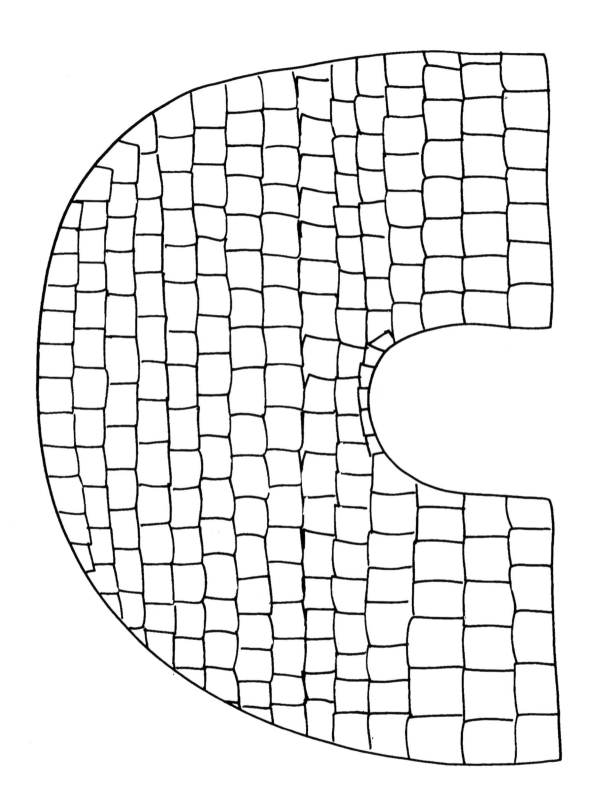

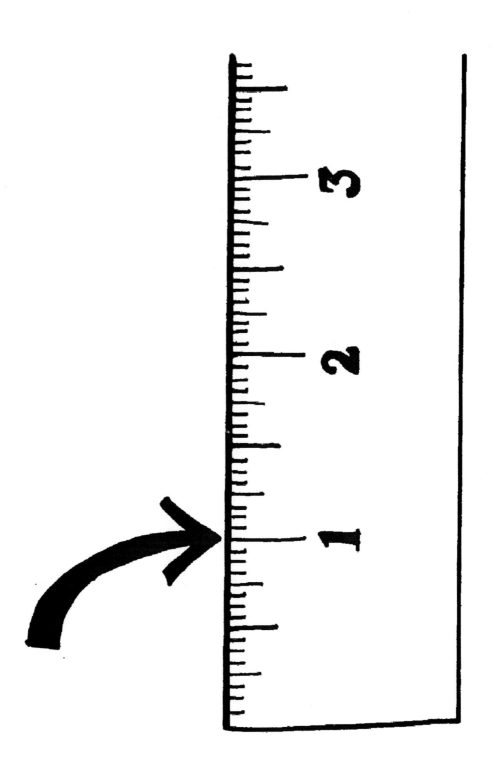

LESSON 3

Objective:

Child will focus on the 4 main cueing systems while reading little book, *My Ii Book.*

Materials:

- Big Book—*My Ii Book*
- Little books—*My Ii Book*
- Awards (see directions p. xii)
- Safety pins

Procedure:

1. Introduce the lesson with the "big book," *My Ii Book.*
2. You read the "big book" with the children, modeling 1-1 match and directionality while pointing to the words.
3. Echo read the book.

INDIVIDUALIZED INSTRUCTION

Note—The objective is to focus the child on the 4 main cueing systems:

- Meaning
- Visual
- Structure
- 1-1 Match

(See page viii for definition and more information.)

1. You now take each child, one at a time, having him/her read the little book, *My Ii Book,* to you. Child points to words while reading.
2. As the child is reading to you, you are listening for misread text and prompting the child with the appropriate question to help him/her correct the error. Your phrasing of the questions must be consistent with those in the "Examples of Misread Text."
3. Through repeated use of these techniques, the children will begin to ask themselves these questions. This indicates the child is now monitoring his/her own reading and is on the way to becoming an independent reader.
4. Following are specific examples of misread text by a child using little *My Ii Book.* Find the type of example that matches what your student has

read. After using the appropriate strategy questions and the child still cannot recall the word, then tell the child the word! Teach the child right from the start that reading is *not* a trick!

5. The child's response may not be an exact match to the example. However, if the response is a similar mistake, prompt the child with the appropriate question.

Examples of Misread Text

Following are specific examples of misread text by a child using little *My Ii Book.* Find the type of example that matches what your student has read. Keep in mind that the child's response may not be an exact match to the example. However, if the response is a similar mistake, prompt the child with the appropriate question.

WHEN TO USE MEANING QUESTIONS

Objective:

Child must determine if what he/she has read makes sense in relation to the picture and in the context of the book he/she is reading.

Example

Child reads:	I see the mountain.
Text reads:	I see the island.

Strategy

Teacher:	"Look at the picture. Is that a mountain?"
Child:	"No. It's an island."
Teacher:	"Good! *Good readers reread.*"

WHEN TO USE STRUCTURE QUESTIONS

Objective:

Child must be able to hear what he/she has read and determine if it sounds right grammatically.

Example

Child reads: I see the ice cream. Eat it good.
Text reads: I see the ice cream. Eat it up!

Strategy

Teacher: "Does that sound right? Is that how people talk?"
Child: "No."
Teacher: "What would sound right?"
Child: "I see the ice cream. Eat it up!"
Teacher: "Good! *Good readers reread.*"

WHEN TO USE VISUAL QUESTIONS

Objective:

Child will use letter in the initial position to read a word in context.

Example

Child reads: I see the rock.
Text reads: I see the island.

Strategy

You point to misread word: "What word do you know that starts with letter i and makes sense?"

Child: "Island."
Teacher: "Reread."
Child: "I see the island."

If the child hesitates and cannot recall the word, give it! Then have the child reread.

WHEN TO USE 1-1 QUESTIONS

Objective:

Child must understand what he/she says has to match the number of words on the page.

Example 1

Child reads: I see the one inch.
Text reads: I see the inch.

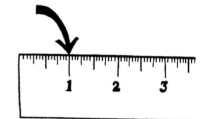

Strategy

Teacher: "Did your finger match the words?"

Child: "No."

Teacher: "Reread."

If the finger does not match the second time, you take the child's finger and point to the words together.

Example 2

Child reads: I see the ice cream. Eat it!
Text reads: I see the ice cream. Eat it up!

Strategy

Teacher: "Did your finger match the words?"

Child: "No."

Teacher: "Reread."

If the child responds, "Yes, my finger did match," take the child's finger and point to the words together.

LETTER Ii AWARD

When the child has successfully read his/her own My Ii Book to you, reward the child with an award. Copy and cut out the one shown here. Pin the award to the child's clothes.

CONCLUSION OF LESSON

Remind the child to leave the award on until a grown-up at home asks him/her to read the book.

LETTER Jj

LESSON 1

Objective:

Child will

∎ visually recognize letter by name.

∎ recognize the sound /j/ in the initial position by naming words with j in that position.

Materials:

∎ Large chart with poem, *Jelly Beans* (see directions on p. x)

∎ Any alphabet card with the letter Jj

∎ Letter Jj can, containing such items as:
  - jelly beans
  - baby food jar
  - toy jeep
  - jumprope
  - jacks

Procedure:

STEP 1

1. Introduce the lesson with the poem, *Jelly Beans.*

2. Display the poem on an easel. You read the poem modeling 1-1 match with a pointer.

Jelly Beans

Jelly beans are fun to eat,
Share them with the friends
you meet.
Eat a few, they sure are yummy.
But... not too many,
They'll hurt your tummy!

3. Ask the whole group, "What letter of the alphabet do you think we are studying now?"
4. Ask children to echo read the poem several times.
5. Ask children for suggestions of movements for acting out the poem.
6. Reread the poem together, acting it out!
7. Put the poem aside.

STEP 2

1. Display the alphabet card with the letter Jj.
2. Ask children to name the letter they see on the alphabet card.
3. Hold up the letter Jj can.
4. Ask children to predict what would make sense in a Jj can.
5. Take each object/picture out of the can. Name them.
6. Ask children to repeat the name of each object/picture after you name it.
7. Show children a sample of the art activity.

8. You now do the art activity with the children, either as a small group or whole class.

ART ACTIVITY

Jelly Beans

Materials:

- Blackline master of poem *Jelly Beans*
- Blackline master of jar and jelly beans
- Crayons
- Blue construction paper 6″ × 9″
- Glue
- Scissors
- Stapler

Preparation:

Reproduce the poem *Jelly Beans* and staple it to the right side of the blue construction paper.

Procedure:

1. Children color the jelly beans.
2. Children cut out jelly beans and jar.
3. With teacher guidance, children glue jelly beans on jar.
4. Let dry.
5. Staple jar of jelly beans to left side of the blue construction paper.
6. Send the poem and art activity home. This gives family members an opportunity to reread the poem with the child, reinforcing the letter Jj.

CONCLUSION OF LESSON

Remind children they have learned to recognize letter Jj and they can think of words that have Jj in the initial position.

Jelly Beans

Jelly beans are fun to eat,

Share them with the friends

you meet.

Eat a few, they sure are

yummy.

But... not too many,

They'll hurt your tummy!

Jelly Beans

Jelly beans are fun to eat,

Share them with the friends

you meet.

Eat a few, they sure are

yummy.

But... not too many,

They'll hurt your tummy!

LESSON 2

Objective:

Children will read *My Jj Book* using 1-1 match.

Materials:

- Big Book—*My Jj Book* (see directions p. xi)
- Large poem—*Jelly Beans* (see directions p. x)
- Little books—*My Jj Book* (see directions p. xi)
- Crayons

Procedure:

1. Introduce the lesson with the poem *Jelly Beans.*
2. You reread the poem *Jelly Beans* modeling 1-1 match with a pointer. Children echo read the poem and act it out.
3. You hold up the "big book," *My Jj Book.* You read the title. Children echo read.
4. You go through each page of the "big book," covering all print. You name the picture on the page. Tell the children to listen for Jj words.
5. You read through the "big book" one time, modeling 1-1 match and directionality.
6. Invite the children to now read the "big book" with you. Model 1-1 match and directionality while reading.
7. The children read through the book a third time while you point to the words.

INDEPENDENT ACTIVITY

1. Reproduce blackline master of the little *My Jj Book.* Give children their own little *My Jj Book* and have them color it in.
2. After children color in their own little *My Jj Book,* they read their book to a partner.
3. You monitor the activity, looking for 1-1 match and directionality.
4. Collect the books.

CONCLUSION OF LESSON

1. You gather the whole group back together for whole group instruction.
2. Everyone rereads the "big book," *My Jj Book,* together.
3. While the children are reading the "big book," you model 1-1 match and directionality, while pointing to the words.

My Jj Book

_____

(name)

The jeep has wheels.

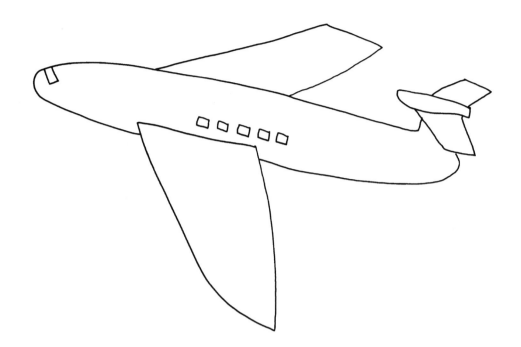

The jet has wings.

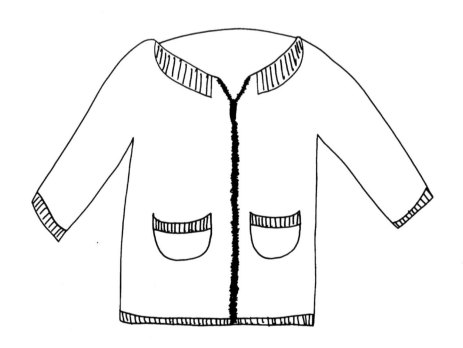

The jacket has pockets.

The jungle has animals.

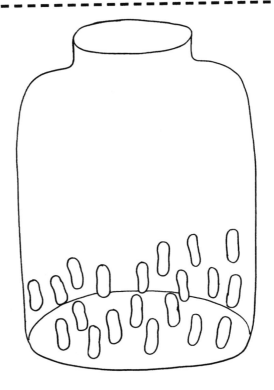

The jar has jelly beans.
How many?

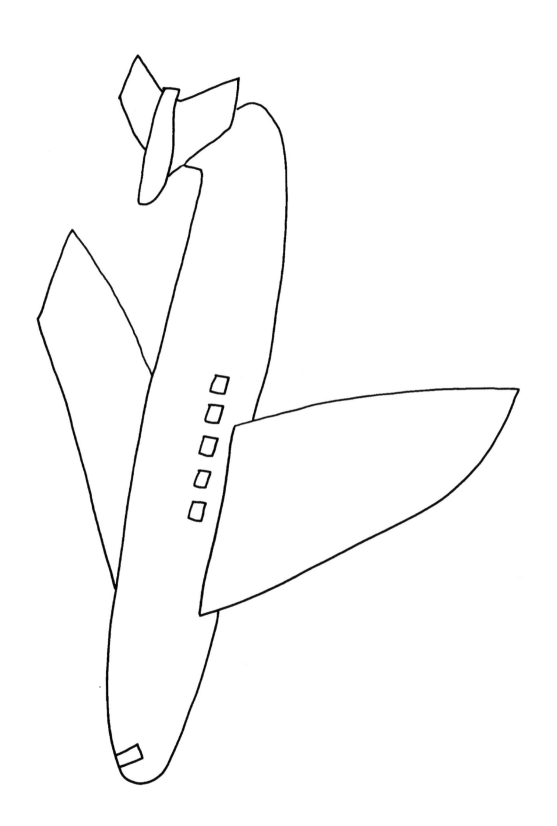

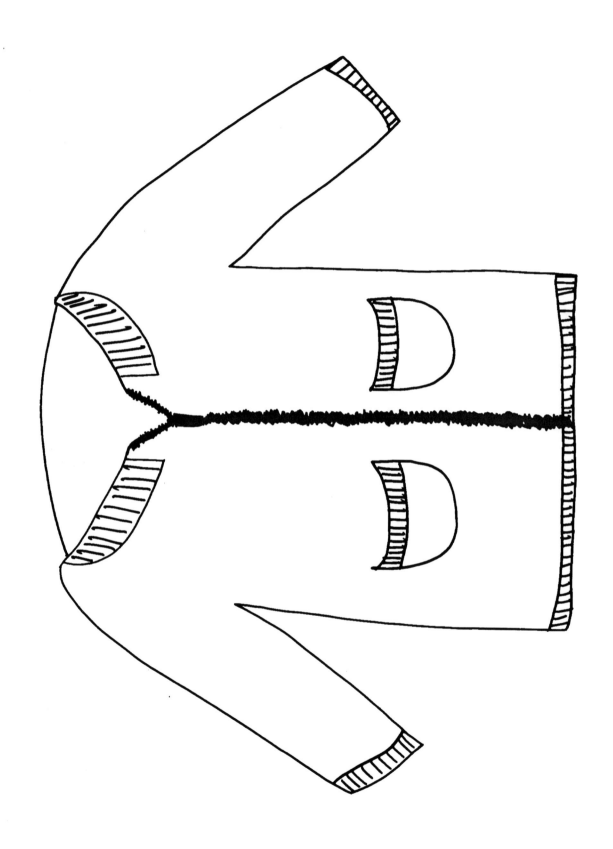

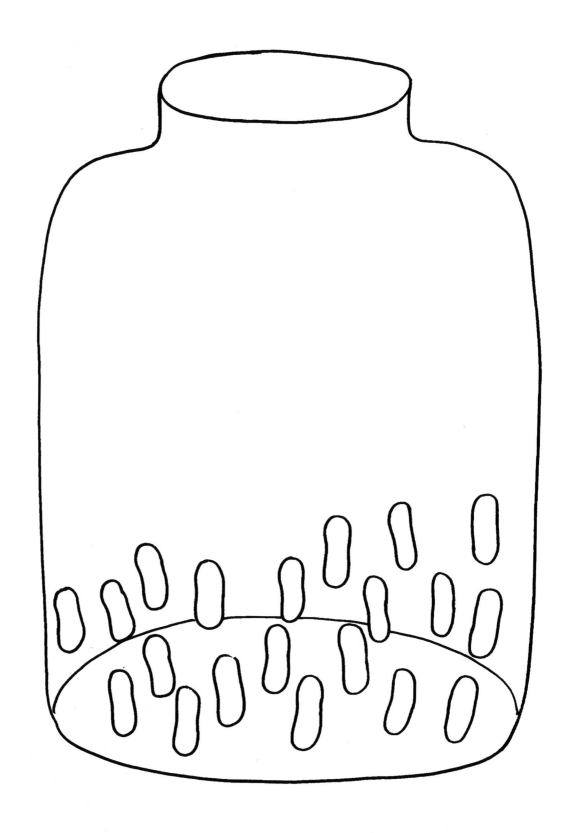

LESSON 3

Objective:

Child will focus on the 4 main cueing systems while reading little book, *My Jj Book.*

Materials:

▮ Big Book—*My Jj Book*
▮ Little books—*My Jj Book*
▮ Awards (see directions p. xii)
▮ Safety pins

Procedure:

1. Introduce the lesson with the "big book," *My Jj Book.*
2. You read the "big book" with the children, modeling 1-1 match and directionality while pointing to the words.
3. Echo read the book.

INDIVIDUALIZED INSTRUCTION

Note—The objective is to focus the child on the 4 main cueing systems:

▮ Meaning
▮ Visual
▮ Structure
▮ 1-1 Match

(See page viii for definition and more information.)

1. You now take each child, one at a time, having him/her read the little book, *My Jj Book* to you. Child points to words while reading.
2. As the child is reading to you, you are listening for misread text and prompting the child with the appropriate question to help him/her correct the error. Your phrasing of the questions must be consistent with those in the "Examples of Misread Text."
3. Through repeated use of these techniques, the children will begin to ask themselves these questions. This indicates the child is now monitoring his/her own reading and is on the way to becoming an independent reader.
4. Following are specific examples of misread text by a child using little *My Jj Book.* Find the type of example that matches what your student has read. After using the appropriate strategy questions and the child still can-

not recall the word, then tell the child the word! Teach the child right from the start that reading is *not* a trick!

5. The child's response may not be an exact match to the example. However, if the response is a similar mistake, prompt the child with the appropriate question.

Examples of Misread Text

Following are specific examples of misread text by a child using little *My Jj Book*. Find the type of example that matches what your student has read. Keep in mind that the child's response may not be an exact match to the example. However, if the response is a similar mistake, prompt the child with the appropriate question.

WHEN TO USE MEANING QUESTIONS

Objective:

Child must determine if what he/she has read makes sense in relation to the picture and in the context of the book he/she is reading.

Example

Child reads: The plane has wings.
Text reads: The jet has wings.

Strategy

Teacher: "Does plane make sense in a Jj book?"

Child: "No."

Teacher: "What else could you try?"

Child: "Jet."

Teacher: "Good! Jet begins with j. *Good readers reread.*"

WHEN TO USE STRUCTURE QUESTIONS

Objective:

Child must be able to hear what he/she has read and determine if it sounds right grammatically.

Example

Child reads: The jeep have wheels.
Text reads: The jeep has wheels.

Strategy

Teacher: "Does that sound right? Is that how people talk?"

Child: "No."

Teacher: "What would sound right?"

Child: "The jeep has wheels."

Teacher: "Good! *Good readers reread.*"

WHEN TO USE VISUAL QUESTIONS

Objective:

Child will use letter in the initial position to read a word in context.

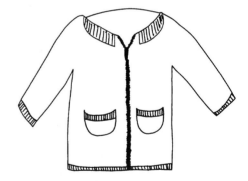

Example

Child reads: The coat has pockets.
Text reads: The jacket has pockets.

Strategy

You point to misread word: "What sound does the letter j make?"

Child: "Jjjj."

Teacher: "Reread."

Child: "The jacket has pockets."

If the child hesitates and cannot recall the word, give it! Then have the child reread.

WHEN TO USE 1-1 QUESTIONS

Objective:

Child must understand what he/she says has to match the number of words on the page.

Example 1

Child reads: The jungle has a lion.
Text reads: The jungle has animals.

Strategy

Teacher: "Did your finger match the words?"

Child: "No."

Teacher: "Reread."

If the finger does not match the second time, you take the child's finger and point to the words together.

Example 2

Child reads: The jar has beans. How many?
Text reads: The jar has jelly beans. How many?

Strategy

Teacher: "Did your finger match the words?"

Child: "No."

Teacher: "Reread."

If the child responds, "Yes, my finger did match," take the child's finger and point to the words together.

LETTER Jj AWARD

When the child has successfully read his/her own *My Jj Book* to you, reward the child with an award. Copy and cut out the one shown here. Pin the award to the child's clothes.

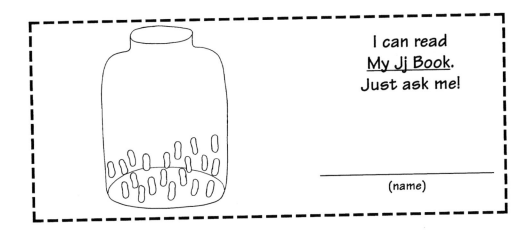

I can read
<u>My Jj Book</u>.
Just ask me!

_____
(name)

<u>CONCLUSION OF LESSON</u>

Remind the child to leave the award on until a grown-up at home asks him/her to read the book.

LETTER Kk

LESSON 1

Objective:

Child will

- visually recognize letter by name.
- recognize the sound /k/ in the initial position by naming words with k in that position.

Materials:

- Large chart with poem, *Kangaroo, Kangaroo* (see directions on p. x)
- Any alphabet card with the letter Kk
- Letter Kk can, containing such items as:
    - magazine picture of koala, kitchen
    - ketchup bottle
    - toy kangaroo
    - keys

Procedure:

STEP 1

1. Introduce the lesson with the poem, *Kangaroo, Kangaroo.*
2. Display the poem on an easel. You read the poem modeling 1-1 match with a pointer.

Kangaroo, Kangaroo

Kangaroo, kangaroo
hop up and down.
Kangaroo, kangaroo
turn around.
You jump so high.
You reach the sky.
Hold your joey tight!

3. Ask the whole group, "What letter of the alphabet do you think we are studying now?"
4. Ask children to echo read the poem several times.
5. Ask children for suggestions of movements for acting out the poem.
6. Reread the poem together, acting it out!
7. Put the poem aside.

STEP 2

1. Display the alphabet card with the letter Kk.
2. Ask children to name the letter they see on the alphabet card.
3. Hold up the letter Kk can.
4. Ask children to predict what would make sense in a Kk can.
5. Take each object/picture out of the can. Name them.
6. Ask children to repeat the name of each object/picture after you name it.
7. Show children a sample of the art activity.
8. You now do the art activity with the children, either as a small group or whole class.

ART ACTIVITY

Kangaroo Mom and Baby

Materials:

- Blackline master of poem *Kangaroo, Kangaroo*
- Blackline master of kangaroo
- Crayons
- Yellow construction paper 12″ × 18″
- Wiggly eyes
- Scissors
- Glue
- Stapler

Preparation:

You staple the poem to the right side of the yellow construction paper.

Procedure:

1. Children color the kangaroo.
2. Use the red crayon for the nose.
3. Children cut out the blackline of the kangaroo.
4. With teacher guidance, children glue wiggly eyes on mommy kangaroo and baby.
5. Let dry.
6. Staple kangaroo to left side of the yellow construction paper.
7. Send the poem and art activity home. This gives family members an opportunity to reread the poem with the child, reinforcing the letter Kk.

CONCLUSION OF LESSON

Remind children they have learned to recognize letter Kk and they can think of words that have Kk in the initial position.

Kangaroo, Kangaroo

Kangaroo, Kangaroo,

hop up and down.

Kangaroo, Kangaroo,

turn around.

You jump so high.

You reach the sky.

Hold your joey tight!

Kangaroo, Kangaroo

Kangaroo, Kangaroo,

hop up and down.

Kangaroo, Kangaroo,

turn around.

You jump so high.

You reach the sky.

Hold your joey tight!

BLACKLINE MASTER—POEM

LESSON 2

Objective:

Children will read *My Kk Book* using 1-1 match.

Materials:

- Big Book—*My Kk Book* (see directions p. xi)
- Large poem—*Kangaroo, Kangaroo* (see directions p. x)
- Little books—*My Kk Book* (see directions p. xi)
- Crayons

Procedure:

1. Introduce the lesson with the poem *Kangaroo, Kangaroo.*
2. You reread the poem *Kangaroo, Kangaroo* modeling 1-1 match with a pointer. Children echo read the poem and act it out.
3. You hold up the "big book," *My Kk Book.* You read the title. Children echo read.
4. You go through each page of the "big book," covering all print. You name the picture on the page. Tell the children to listen for Kk words.
5. You read through the "big book" one time, modeling 1-1 match and directionality.
6. Invite the children to now read the "big book" with you. Model 1-1 match and directionality while reading.
7. The children read through the book a third time while you point to the words.

INDEPENDENT ACTIVITY

1. Reproduce blackline master of the little *My Kk Book.* Give children their own little *My Kk Book* and have them color it in.
2. After children color in their own little *My Kk Book,* they read their book to a partner.
3. You monitor the activity, looking for 1-1 match and directionality.
4. Collect the books.

CONCLUSION OF LESSON

1. You gather the whole group back together for whole group instruction.
2. Everyone rereads the "big book," *My Kk Book,* together.
3. While the children are reading the "big book," you model 1-1 match and directionality, while pointing to the words.

My Kk Book

_____
(name)

Can you see the kangaroo?

Can you see the king?

- -

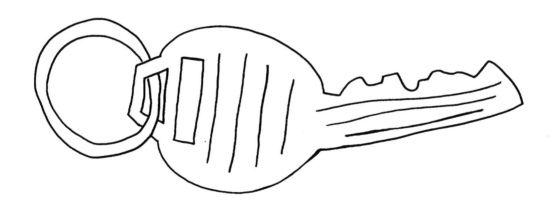

Can you see the key?

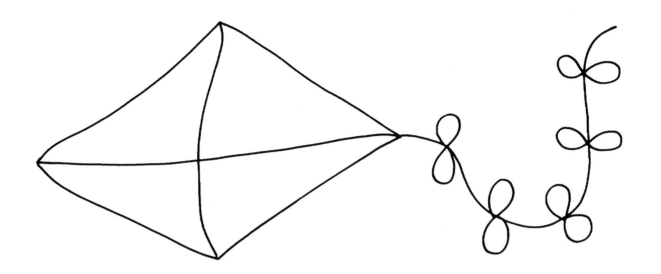

Can you see the kite?

Can you see the kid hiding?
Yes!

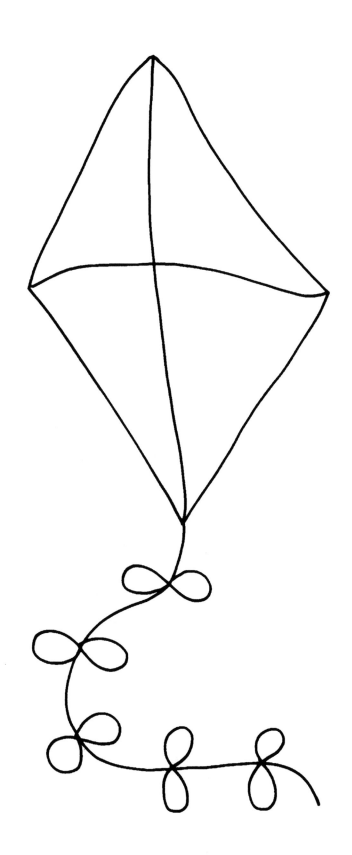

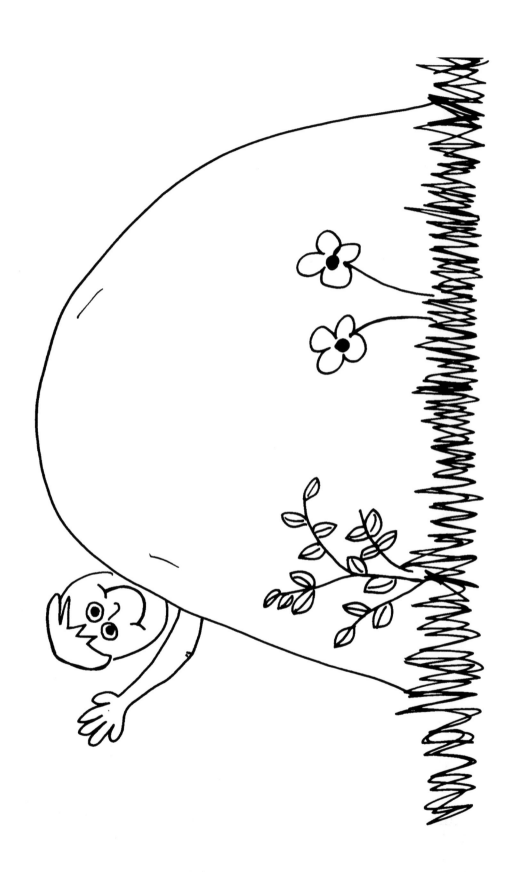

LESSON 3

Objective:

Child will focus on the 4 main cueing systems while reading little book, *My Kk Book.*

Materials:

■ Big Book—*My Kk Book*
■ Little books—*My Kk Book*
■ Awards (see directions p. xii)
■ Safety pins

Procedure:

1. Introduce the lesson with the "big book," *My Kk Book.*
2. You read the "big book" with the children, modeling 1-1 match and directionality while pointing to the words.
3. Echo read the book.

INDIVIDUALIZED INSTRUCTION

Note—The objective is to focus the child on the 4 main cueing systems:

■ Meaning
■ Visual
■ Structure
■ 1-1 Match

(See page viii for definition and more information.)

1. You now take each child, one at a time, having him/her read the little book, *My Kk Book,* to you. Child points to words while reading.
2. As the child is reading to you, you are listening for misread text and prompting the child with the appropriate question to help him/her correct the error. Your phrasing of the questions must be consistent with those in the "Examples of Misread Text."
3. Through repeated use of these techniques, the children will begin to ask themselves these questions. This indicates the child is now monitoring his/her own reading and is on the way to becoming an independent reader.
4. Following are specific examples of misread text by a child using little *My Kk Book.* Find the type of example that matches what your student has

read. After using the appropriate strategy questions and the child still cannot recall the word, then tell the child the word! Teach the child right from the start that reading is *not* a trick!

5. The child's response may not be an exact match to the example. However, if the response is a similar mistake, prompt the child with the appropriate question.

Examples of Misread Text

Following are specific examples of misread text by a child using little *My Kk Book.* Find the type of example that matches what your student has read. Keep in mind that the child's response may not be an exact match to the example. However, if the response is a similar mistake, prompt the child with the appropriate question.

WHEN TO USE MEANING QUESTIONS

Objective:

Child must determine if what he/she has read makes sense in relation to the picture and in the context of the book he/she is reading.

Example

Child reads: Can you see the lady?
Text reads: Can you see the kid hiding? Yes!

Strategy

Teacher: "Look at the picture. Is that a lady?"
Child: "No. It's a kid."
Teacher: "Good! *Good readers reread.*"

WHEN TO USE STRUCTURE QUESTIONS

Objective:

Child must be able to hear what he/she has read and determine if it sounds right grammatically.

Example

| Child reads: | Can you see they kite? |
| Text reads: | Can you see the kite? |

Strategy

Teacher:	"Does that sound right? Is that how people talk?"
Child:	"No."
Teacher:	"What would sound right?"
Child:	"Can you see the kite?"
Teacher:	"Good! *Good readers reread.*"

WHEN TO USE VISUAL QUESTIONS

Objective:

Child will use letter in the initial position to read a word in context.

Example

| Child reads: | Can you see the prince? |
| Text reads: | Can you see the king? |

Strategy

Teacher:	"What sound does the letter k make?"
Child:	"Kkkk."
Teacher:	"Reread."
Child:	"Can you see the king?"

If the child hesitates and cannot recall the word, give it! Then have the child reread.

WHEN TO USE 1-1 QUESTIONS

Objective:

Child must understand what he/she says has to match the number of words on the page.

Example 1

Child reads: Can you see the kite fly?
Text reads: Can you see the kite?

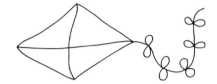

Strategy

Teacher: "Did your finger match the words?"

Child: "No."

Teacher: "Reread."

If the finger does not match the second time, you take the child's finger and point to the words together.

Example 2

Child reads: Can you see the kid hiding?
Text reads: Can you see the kid hiding? Yes!

Strategy

Teacher: "Did your finger match the words?"

Child: "No."

Teacher: "Reread."

If the child responds, "Yes, my finger did match," take the child's finger and point to the words together.

LETTER Kk AWARD

When the child has successfully read his/her own *My Kk Book* to you, reward the child with an award. Copy and cut out the one shown here. Pin the award to the child's clothes.

I can read
My Kk Book.
Just ask me!

_____
(name)

<u>CONCLUSION OF LESSON</u>

Remind the child to leave the award on until a grown-up at home asks him/her to read the book.

 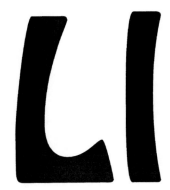

LETTER

LESSON 1

Objective:

Child will

- visually recognize letter by name.
- recognize the sound /l/ in the initial position by naming words with l in that position.

Materials:

- Large chart with poem, *The Lion* (see directions on p. x)
- Any alphabet card with the letter Ll
- Letter Ll can, containing such items as:
    - magazine picture of lamb
    - toy lion
    - lipstick
    - plastic lemon
    - lollipop

Procedure:

STEP 1

1. Introduce the lesson with the poem, *The Lion.*
2. Display the poem on an easel. You read the poem modeling 1-1 match with a pointer.

The Lion

The lion roams the plain.
Swinging his tail,
and tossing his mane.
Hunting for food,
by stalking his prey.
He has no time to run and play.
His walk is oh, so strong and proud.
And when he roars,
He's very loud!

3. Ask the whole group, "What letter of the alphabet do you think we are studying now?"
4. Ask children to echo read the poem several times.
5. Ask children for suggestions of movements for acting out the poem.
6. Reread the poem together, acting it out!
7. Put the poem aside.

STEP 2

1. Display the alphabet card with the letter Ll.
2. Ask children to name the letter they see on the alphabet card.
3. Hold up the letter Ll can.
4. Ask children to predict what would make sense in an Ll can.
5. Take each object/picture out of the can. Name them.
6. Ask children to repeat the name of each object/picture after you name it.
7. Show children a sample of the art activity.

8. You now do the art activity with the children, either as a small group or whole class.

ART ACTIVITY

Leapin' Lions

Materials:

- Blackline master of poem *The Lion*
- Blackline master of lion
- Crayons—orange and black
- Black construction paper 12″ × 18″
- Scissors
- Pencils
- Stapler

Preparation:

Reproduce the poem *The Lion* and staple it to the right side of the black construction paper.

Procedure:

1. Children color the mane of the lion using orange crayons.
2. Children color the nose using black crayons.
3. Children cut out the blackline of the lion.
4. With teacher guidance, children cut the lines of the mane.
5. With teacher guidance, children use pencils to wrap each strip of mane around the pencil and roll it.
6. Staple lion to left side of the black construction paper.
7. Send the poem and art activity home. This gives family members an opportunity to reread the poem with the child, reinforcing the letter Ll.

CONCLUSION OF LESSON

Remind children they have learned to recognize letter Ll and they can think of words that have Ll in the initial position.

The Lion

The lion roams on the plain.

Swinging his tail, and
tossing his mane.

Hunting for food, by
stalking his prey.

He has no time to run
and play.

His walk is oh, so strong
and proud.

And when he roars,
he's very loud!

The Lion

The lion roams on the plain.

Swinging his tail, and
tossing his mane.

Hunting for food, by
stalking his prey.

He has no time to run
and play.

His walk is oh, so strong
and proud.

And when he roars,
he's very loud!

LESSON 2

Objective:

Children will read *My Ll Book* using 1-1 match.

Materials:

- Big Book—*My Ll Book* (see directions p. xi)
- Large poem—*Lion* (see directions p.x)
- Little books—*My Ll Book* (see directions p. xi)
- Crayons

Procedure:

1. Introduce the lesson with the poem *The Lion.*
2. You reread the poem *The Lion* modeling 1-1 match with a pointer. Children echo read the poem and act it out.
3. You hold up the "big book," *My Ll Book.* You read the title. Children echo read.
4. You go through each page of the "big book," covering all print. You name the picture on the page. Tell the children to listen for Ll words.
5. You read through the "big book" one time, modeling 1-1 match and directionality.
6. Invite the children to now read the "big book" with you. Model 1-1 match and directionality while reading.
7. The children read through the book a third time while you point to the words.

INDEPENDENT ACTIVITY

1. Reproduce blackline master of the little *My Ll Book.* Give children their own little *My Ll Book* and have them color it in.
2. After children color in their own little *My Ll Book,* they read their book to a partner.
3. You monitor the activity, looking for 1-1 match and directionality.
4. Collect the books.

CONCLUSION OF LESSON

1. You gather the whole group back together for whole group instruction.
2. Everyone rereads the "big book," *My Ll Book,* together.
3. While the children are reading the "big book," you model 1-1 match and directionality, while pointing to the words.

My Ll Book

_____
(name)

- -

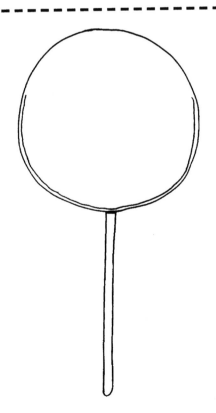

I see the lollipop.

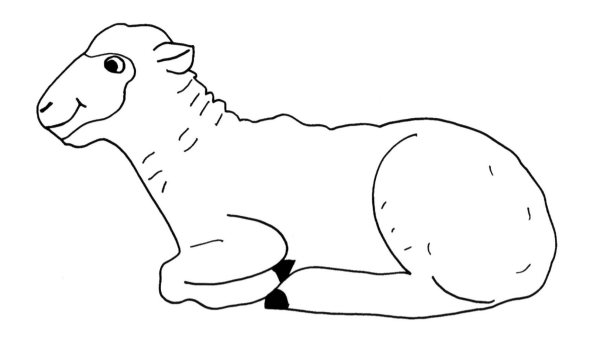

I see the lamb.

I see the lips.

I see the lion.

I see the ladder. Climb it!

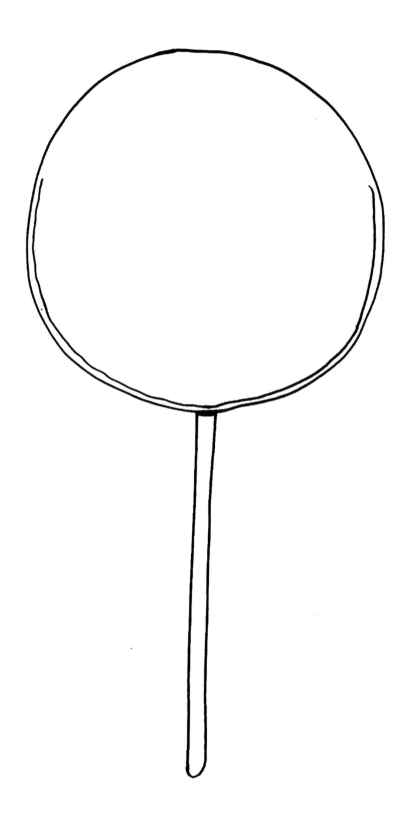

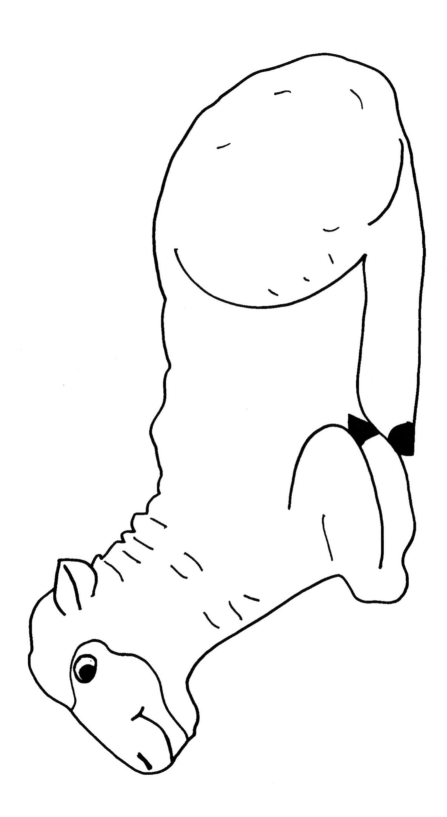

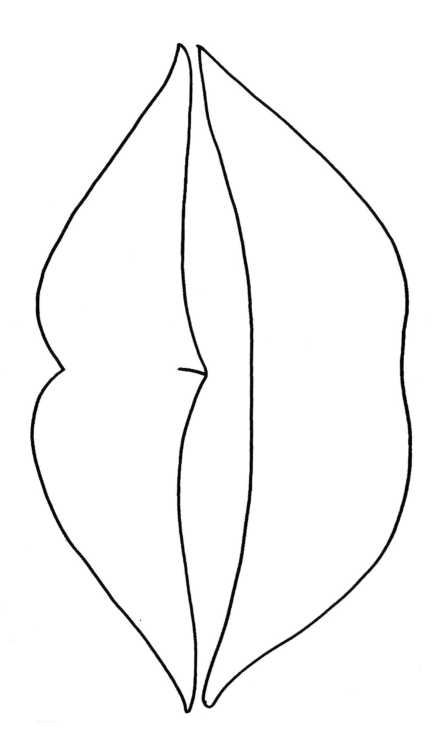

LESSON 3

Objective:

Child will focus on the 4 main cueing systems while reading little book, *My Ll Book.*

Materials:

▪ Big Book—*My Ll Book*
▪ Little books—*My Ll Book*
▪ Awards (see directions p. xii)
▪ Safety pins

Procedure:

1. Introduce the lesson with the "big book," *My Ll Book.*
2. You read the "big book" with the children, modeling 1-1 match and directionality while pointing to the words.
3. Echo read the book.

INDIVIDUALIZED INSTRUCTION

Note—The objective is to focus the child on the 4 main cueing systems:

▪ Meaning
▪ Visual
▪ Structure
▪ 1-1 Match

(See page viii for definition and more information.)

1. You now take each child, one at a time, having him/her read the little book, *My Ll Book* to you. Child points to words while reading.
2. As the child is reading to you, you are listening for misread text and prompting the child with the appropriate question to help him/her correct the error. Your phrasing of the questions must be consistent with those in the "Examples of Misread Text."
3. Through repeated use of these techniques, the children will begin to ask themselves these questions. This indicates the child is now monitoring his/her own reading and is on the way to becoming an independent reader.
4. Following are specific examples of misread text by a child using little *My Ll Book.* Find the type of example that matches what your student has read. After using the appropriate strategy questions and the child still can-

not recall the word, then tell the child the word! Teach the child right from the start that reading is *not* a trick!

5. The child's response may not be an exact match to the example. However, if the response is a similar mistake, prompt the child with the appropriate question.

Examples of Misread Text

Following are specific examples of misread text by a child using little *My Ll Book.* Find the type of example that matches what your student has read. Keep in mind that the child's response may not be an exact match to the example. However, if the response is a similar mistake, prompt the child with the appropriate question.

WHEN TO USE MEANING QUESTIONS

Objective:

Child must determine if what he/she has read makes sense in relation to the picture and in the context of the book he/she is reading.

Example

Child reads: I see the balloon.
Text reads: I see the lollipop.

Strategy

Teacher:	"Does balloon make sense in an Ll book?"
Child:	"No."
Teacher:	"What else could you try?"
Child:	"Lollipop."
Teacher:	"Good! Lollipop begins with l. *Good readers reread.*"

WHEN TO USE STRUCTURE QUESTIONS

Objective:

Child must be able to hear what he/she has read and determine if it sounds right grammatically.

Example

Child reads: A see the ladder.
Text reads: I see the ladder.

Strategy

Teacher:	"Does that sound right? Is that how people talk?"
Child:	"No."
Teacher:	"What would sound right?"
Child:	"I see the ladder."
Teacher:	"Good! *Good readers reread.*"

WHEN TO USE VISUAL QUESTIONS

Objective:

Child will use letter in the initial position to read a word in context.

Example

Child reads: I see the mouth.
Text reads: I see the lips.

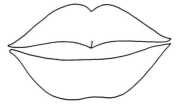

Strategy

Teacher:	"What sound does the letter l make?"
Child:	"Llll."
Teacher:	"Reread."
Child:	"I see the lips."

If the child hesitates and cannot recall the word, give it! Then have the child reread.

WHEN TO USE 1-1 QUESTIONS

Objective:

Child must understand what he/she says has to match the number of words on the page.

Example 1

Child reads: I see the big ladder.
Text reads: I see the ladder.

Strategy

Teacher: "Did your finger match the words?"

Child: "No."

Teacher: "Reread."

If the finger does not match the second time, you take the child's finger and point to the words together.

Example 2

Child reads: See the lollipop.
Text reads: I see the lollipop.

Strategy

Teacher: "Did your finger match the words?"

Child: "No."

Teacher: "Reread."

If the child responds, "Yes, my finger did match," take the child's finger and point to the words together.

LETTER Ll AWARD

When the child has successfully read his/her own *My Ll Book* to you, reward the child with an award. Copy and cut out the one shown here. Pin the award to the child's clothes.

I can read
My Ll Book.
Just ask me!

_____
(name)

CONCLUSION OF LESSON

Remind the child to leave the award on until a grown-up at home asks him/her to read the book.

LETTER

LESSON 1

Objective:

Child will

∎ visually recognize letter by name.

∎ recognize the sound /m/ in the initial position by naming words with m in that position.

Materials:

∎ Large chart with poem, *Monkeys* (see directions on p. x)

∎ Any alphabet card with the letter Mm

∎ Letter Mm can, containing such items as:
 – miniature toy monkey, mouse
 – money
 – mitten
 – M & M's

Procedure:

STEP 1

1. Introduce the lesson with the poem, *Monkeys*.

2. Display the poem on an easel. You read the poem modeling 1-1 match with a pointer.

231

Monkeys

Monkeys swing,
Monkeys climb,
Monkeys jump from vine to vine.
The banana he wants is up the tree,
Get it monkey,
For you and *me*!

3. Ask the whole group, "What letter of the alphabet do you think we are studying now?"
4. Ask children to echo read the poem several times.
5. Ask children for suggestions of movements for acting out the poem.
6. Reread the poem together, acting it out!
7. Put the poem aside.

STEP 2

1. Display the alphabet card with the letter Mm.
2. Ask children to name the letter they see on the alphabet card.
3. Hold up the letter Mm can.
4. Ask children to predict what would make sense in an Mm can.
5. Take each object/picture out of the can. Name them.
6. Ask children to repeat the name of each object/picture after you name it.
7. Show children a sample of the art activity.
8. You now do the art activity with the children, either as a small group or whole class.

ART ACTIVITY

Stuffed Monkey Heads

Materials:

- Blackline master of poem *Monkeys*
- Blackline master of monkey head
- Crayons
- Extra white paper, 8-1/2″ × 11″
- Scissors
- Yellow construction paper 12″ × 18″
- 4 bags of polyfill per class of 20
- Stapler

Preparation:

Reproduce the poem *Monkeys* and staple it to the right side of the yellow construction paper. You staple the monkey head and one sheet of paper together (one set for each child). Staples are placed all around the monkey's outline, leaving an opening for stuffing.

Procedure:

1. Children color monkey head.
2. Children cut it out on the outside of the staples around the monkey's head.
3. Children stuff their monkey head.
4. You staple the rest of the head.
5. The monkey head is stapled to the construction paper.
6. Send the poem and art activity home. This gives family members an opportunity to reread the poem with the child, reinforcing the letter Mm.

CONCLUSION OF LESSON

Remind children they have learned to recognize letter Mm and they can think of words that have Mm in the initial position.

Monkeys

Monkeys swing,

Monkeys climb,

Monkeys jump,

from vine to vine.

The banana he wants,

is up the tree.

Get it, monkey,

For you and me!

Monkeys

Monkeys swing,

Monkeys climb,

Monkeys jump,

from vine to vine.

The banana he wants,

is up the tree.

Get it, monkey,

For you and me!

BLACKLINE MASTER—POEM

BLACKLINE MASTER—MONKEY HEAD

LESSON 2

Objective:

Children will read *My Mm Book* using 1-1 match.

Materials:

- Big Book—*My Mm Book* (see directions p. xi)
- Large poem—*Monkeys* (see directions p. x)
- Little books—*My Mm Book* (see directions p. xi)
- Crayons

Procedure:

1. Introduce the lesson with the poem *Monkeys*.
2. You reread the poem *Monkeys* modeling 1-1 match with a pointer. Children echo read the poem and act it out.
3. You hold up the "big book," *My Mm Book*. You read the title. Children echo read.
4. You go through each page of the "big book," covering all print. You name the picture on the page. Tell the children to listen for Mm words.
5. You read through the "big book" one time, modeling 1-1 match and directionality.
6. Invite the children to now read the "big book" with you. Model 1-1 match and directionality while reading.
7. The children read through the book a third time while you point to the words.

INDEPENDENT ACTIVITY

1. Reproduce blackline master of the little *My Mm Book*. Give children their own little *My Mm Book* and have them color it in.
2. After children color in their own little *My Mm Book*, they read their book to a partner.
3. You monitor the activity, looking for 1-1 match and directionality.
4. Collect the books.

CONCLUSION OF LESSON

1. You gather the whole group back together for whole group instruction.
2. Everyone rereads the "big book," *My Mm Book*, together.
3. While the children are reading the "big book," you model 1-1 match and directionality, while pointing to the words.

My Mm Book

_____
(name)

- -

Look at the monkey.

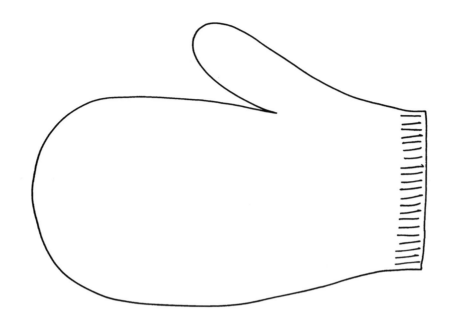

Look at the mitten.

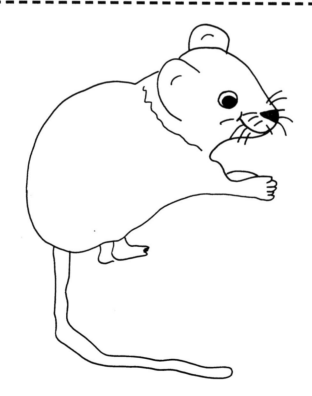

Look at the mouse.

Look at the moon.

Look at the monster. OH NO!

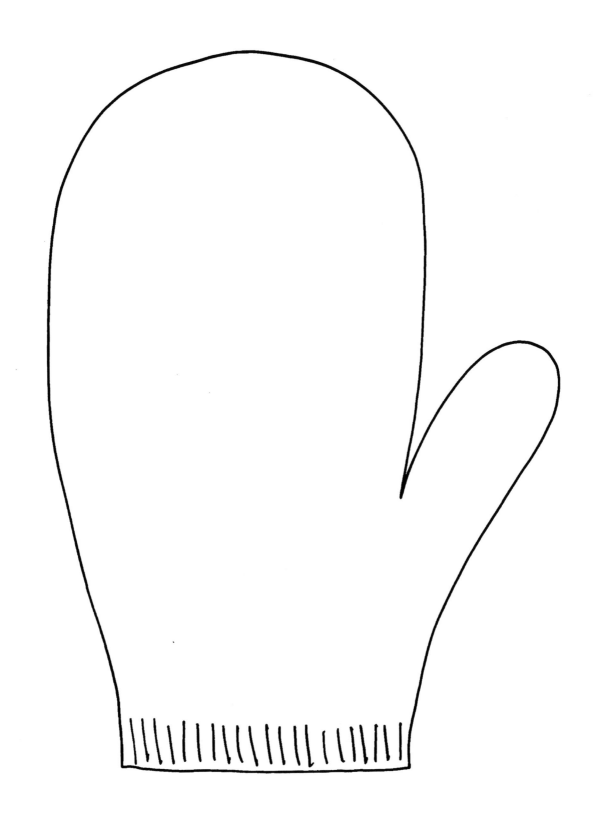

BLACKLINE MASTER—BIG BOOK

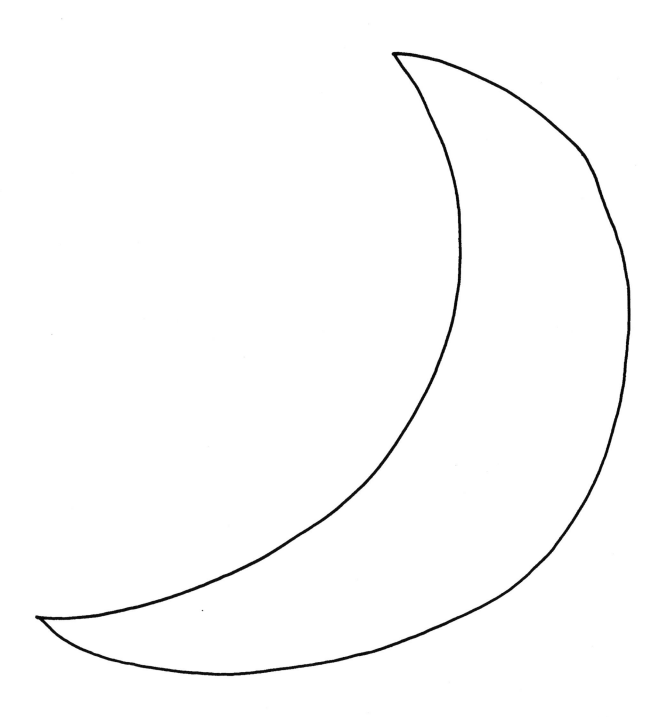

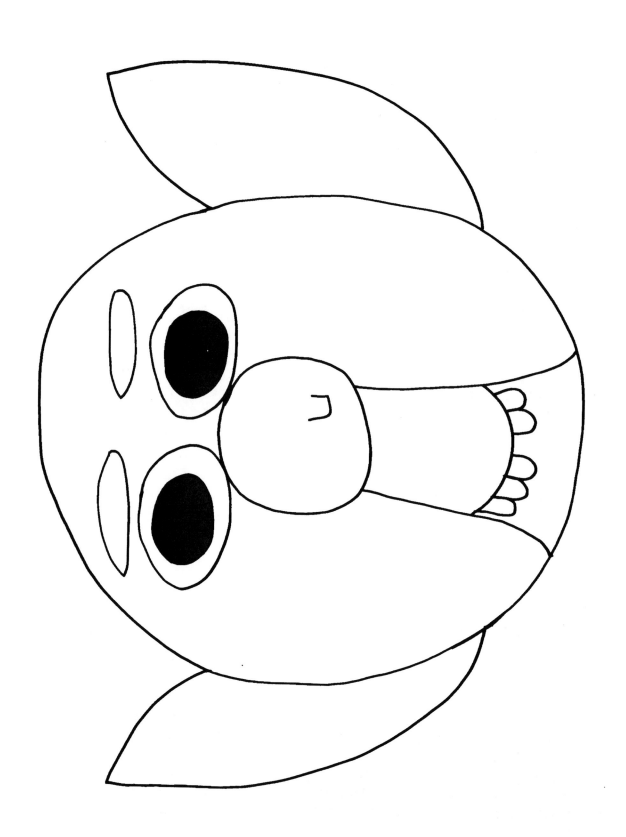

LESSON 3

Objective:

Child will focus on the 4 main cueing systems while reading little book, *My Mm Book.*

Materials:

▪ Big Book—My Mm Book
▪ Little books—My Mm Book
▪ Awards (see directions p. xii)
▪ Safety pins

Procedure:

1. Introduce the lesson with the "big book," *My Mm Book.*
2. You read the "big book" with the children, modeling 1-1 match and directionality while pointing to the words.
3. Echo read the book.

INDIVIDUALIZED INSTRUCTION

Note—The objective is to focus the child on the 4 main cueing systems:

▪ Meaning
▪ Visual
▪ Structure
▪ 1-1 Match

(See page viii for definition and more information.)

1. You now take each child, one at a time, having him/her read the little book, *My Mm Book* to you. Child points to words while reading.
2. As the child is reading to you, you are listening for misread text and prompting the child with the appropriate question to help him/her correct the error. Your phrasing of the questions must be consistent with those in the "Examples of Misread Text."
3. Through repeated use of these techniques, the children will begin to ask themselves these questions. This indicates the child is now monitoring his/her own reading and is on the way to becoming an independent reader.
4. Following are specific examples of misread text by a child using little *My Mm Book.* Find the type of example that matches what your student has

read. After using the appropriate strategy questions and the child still cannot recall the word, then tell the child the word! Teach the child right from the start that reading is *not* a trick!

5. The child's response may not be an exact match to the example. However, if the response is a similar mistake, prompt the child with the appropriate question.

Examples of Misread Text

Following are specific examples of misread text by a child using little *My Mm Book*. Find the type of example that matches what your student has read. Keep in mind that the child's response may not be an exact match to the example. However, if the response is a similar mistake, prompt the child with the appropriate question.

WHEN TO USE MEANING QUESTIONS

Objective:

Child must determine if what he/she has read makes sense in relation to the picture and in the context of the book he/she is reading.

Example

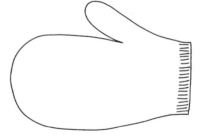

Child reads: Look at the glove.
Text reads: Look at the mitten.

Strategy

Teacher:	"Look at the picture, is that a glove?"
Child:	"No. It's a mitten."
Teacher:	"Good! *Good readers reread.*"

WHEN TO USE STRUCTURE QUESTIONS

Objective:

Child must be able to hear what he/she has read and determine if it sounds right grammatically.

Letter Mm

Example

Child reads: Look and the monkey.
Text reads: Look at the monkey.

Strategy

Teacher: "Does that sound right? Is that how people talk?"

Child: "No."

Teacher: "What would sound right?"

Child: "Look at the monkey."

Teacher: "Good! *Good readers reread.*"

WHEN TO USE VISUAL QUESTIONS

Objective:

Child will use letter in the initial position to read a word in context.

Example

Child reads: Look at the creature.
Text reads: Look at the monster.

Strategy

You point to the misread word: "What sound does the letter m make?"

Child: "Mmm."

Teacher: "Reread."

Child: "Look at the monster."

If the child hesitates and cannot recall the word, give it! Then have the child reread.

WHEN TO USE 1-1 QUESTIONS

Objective:

Child must understand what he/she says has to match the number of words on the page.

Example 1

Child reads: Look at the big moon.
Text reads: Look at the moon.

Strategy

Teacher: "Did your finger match the words?"

Child: "No."

Teacher: "Reread."

If the finger does not match the second time, you take the child's finger and point to the words together.

Example 2

Child reads: Look the moon.
Text reads: Look at the moon.

Strategy

Teacher: "Did your finger match the words?"

Child: "No."

Teacher: "Reread."

If the child responds, "Yes, my finger did match," take the child's finger and point to the words together.

LETTER Mm AWARD

When the child has successfully read his/her own *My Mm Book* to you, reward the child with an award. Copy and cut out the one shown here. Pin the award to the child's clothes.

<u>CONCLUSION OF LESSON</u>

Remind the child to leave the award on until a grown-up at home asks him/her to read the book.

LETTER Nn

LESSON 1

Objective:

Child will

▪ visually recognize letter by name.

▪ recognize the sound /n/ in the initial position by naming words with n in that position.

Materials:

▪ Large chart with poem, *The Best Nest* (see directions on p. x)

▪ Any alphabet card with the letter Nn

▪ Letter Nn can, containing such items as:

– nuts
– newspaper
– nail polish
– nickel
– necklace

Procedure:

STEP 1

1. Introduce the lesson with the poem, *The Best Nest.*

2. Display the poem on an easel. You read the poem modeling 1-1 match with a pointer.

The Best Nest

A nest is a home for a bird in a tree.
She works hard to build it,
where none can see.
In her beak she gathers, sticks
and strings.
She weaves them together,
while she sings.
"Cheep, cheep," say the birds,
as they sit in their nest.
We love our nest,
Our nest is best!

3. Ask the whole group, "What letter of the alphabet do you think we are studying now?"
4. Ask children to echo read the poem several times.
5. Ask children for suggestions of movements for acting out the poem.
6. Reread the poem together, acting it out!
7. Put the poem aside.

STEP 2

1. Display the alphabet card with the letter Nn.
2. Ask children to name the letter they see on the alphabet card.
3. Hold up the letter Nn can.
4. Ask children to predict what would make sense in an Nn can.
5. Take each object/picture out of the can. Name them.
6. Ask children to repeat the name of each object/picture after you name it.
7. Show children a sample of the art activity.
8. You now do the art activity with the children, either as a small group or whole class.

ART ACTIVITY

The Best Nest

Materials:
- Blackline master of poem *The Best Nest*
- Blackline master of bird
- Crayons
- Light blue construction paper 12″ × 18″
- Approximately 20 1/2″-wide × 6″-long brown construction paper strips per child
- Glue
- Scissors
- Stapler

Preparation:

Reproduce the poem *The Best Nest* and staple it to the right side of the light blue construction paper.

Procedure:
1. Children color the bird, then cut it out.
2. With teacher guidance, children glue on 1/2″ brown strips to light blue paper to form a nest.
3. Glue bird in the center of the nest.
4. Let dry.
5. Staple or glue bird in nest to left side of the light blue construction paper.
6. Send the poem and art activity home. This gives family members an opportunity to reread the poem with the child, reinforcing the letter Nn.

CONCLUSION OF LESSON

Remind children they have learned to recognize letter Nn and they can think of words that have Nn in the initial position.

The Best Nest

A nest is a home, for a bird in

a tree. She works hard to

build it, where none can see.

In her beak she gathers,

sticks and strings.

She weaves them together,

while she sings.

"Cheep, cheep," say the birds,

as they sit in their nest.

We love our nest,

Our nest is best!

The Best Nest

A nest is a home, for a bird in

a tree. She works hard to

build it, where none can see.

In her beak she gathers, sticks

and strings.

She weaves them together,

while she sings.

"Cheep, cheep," say the birds,

as they sit in their nest.

We love our nest,

Our nest is best!

BLACKLINE MASTER—POEM

BLACKLINE MASTER—BIRD

LESSON 2

Objective:

Children will read *My Nn Book* using 1-1 match.

Materials:

▪ Big Book—*My Nn Book* (see directions p. xi)
▪ Large poem—*The Best Nest* (see directions p. x)
▪ Little books—*My Nn Book* (see directions p. xi)
▪ Crayons

Procedure:

1. Introduce the lesson with the poem *The Best Nest.*
2. You reread the poem *The Best Nest* modeling 1-1 match with a pointer. Children echo read the poem and act it out.
3. You hold up the "big book," *My Nn Book.* You read the title. Children echo read.
4. You go through each page of the "big book," covering all print. You name the picture on the page. Tell the children to listen for Nn words.
5. You read through the "big book" one time, modeling 1-1 match and directionality.
6. Invite the children to now read the "big book" with you. Model 1-1 match and directionality while reading.
7. The children read through the book a third time while you point to the words.

INDEPENDENT ACTIVITY

1. Reproduce blackline master of the little *My Nn Book.* Give children their own little *My Nn Book* and have them color it in.
2. After children color in their own little *My Nn Book,* they read their book to a partner.
3. You monitor the activity, looking for 1-1 match and directionality.
4. Collect the books.

CONCLUSION OF LESSON

1. You gather the whole group back together for whole group instruction.
2. Everyone rereads the "big book," *My Nn Book,* together.
3. While the children are reading the "big book," you model 1-1 match and directionality, while pointing to the words.

My Nn Book

_____
(name)

The man has a nose.

The giraffe has a long neck.
So long!

The squirrel has a nut.

The girl has a net.

- -

The bird has a nest.

BLACKLINE MASTER—BIG BOOK

LESSON 3

Objective:

Child will focus on the 4 main cueing systems while reading little book, *My Nn Book.*

Materials:

▌ Big Book—*My Nn Book*
▌ Little books—*My Nn Book*
▌ Awards (see directions p. xii)
▌ Safety pins

Procedure:

1. Introduce the lesson with the "big book," *My Nn Book.*
2. You read the "big book" with the children, modeling 1-1 match and directionality while pointing to the words.
3. Echo read the book.

INDIVIDUALIZED INSTRUCTION

Note—The objective is to focus the child on the 4 main cueing systems:

▌ Meaning
▌ Visual
▌ Structure
▌ 1-1 Match

(See page viii for definition and more information.)

1. You now take each child, one at a time, having him/her read the little book, *My Nn Book* to you. Child points to words while reading.
2. As the child is reading to you, you are listening for misread text and prompting the child with the appropriate question to help him/her correct the error. Your phrasing of the questions must be consistent with those in the "Examples of Misread Text."
3. Through repeated use of these techniques, the children will begin to ask themselves these questions. This indicates the child is now monitoring his/her own reading and is on the way to becoming an independent reader.
4. Following are specific examples of misread text by a child using little *My Nn Book.* Find the type of example that matches what your student has read. After using the appropriate strategy questions and the child still

cannot recall the word, then tell the child the word! Teach the child right from the start that reading is *not* a trick!

5. The child's response may not be an exact match to the example. However, if the response is a similar mistake, prompt the child with the appropriate question.

Examples of Misread Text

Following are specific examples of misread text by a child using little *My Nn Book.* Find the type of example that matches what your student has read. Keep in mind that the child's response may not be an exact match to the example. However, if the response is a similar mistake, prompt the child with the appropriate question.

WHEN TO USE MEANING QUESTIONS

Objective:

Child must determine if what he/she has read makes sense in relation to the picture and in the context of the book he/she is reading.

Example

Child reads:	The man has a face.
Text reads:	The man has a nose.

Strategy

Teacher:	"Does face make sense in an Nn book?"
Child:	"No."
Teacher:	"What else could you try?"
Child:	"Nose."
Teacher:	"Good! Nose begins with n. *Good readers reread.*"

WHEN TO USE STRUCTURE QUESTIONS

Objective:

Child must be able to hear what he/she has read and determine if it sounds right grammatically.

Example

Child reads: The girl have a net.
Text reads: The girl has a net.

Strategy

Teacher:	"Does that sound right? Is that how people talk?"
Child:	"No."
Teacher:	"What would sound right?"
Child:	"The girl has a net."
Teacher:	"Good! *Good readers reread.*"

WHEN TO USE VISUAL QUESTIONS

Objective:
Child will use letter in the initial position to read a word in context.

Example

Child reads: The squirrel has a peanut.
Text reads: The squirrel has a nut.

Strategy

You point to the misread word: "What sound does the letter n make?"

Child:	"Nnn."
Teacher:	"Reread."
Child:	"The squirrel has a nut."

If the child hesitates and cannot recall the word, give it! Then have the child reread.

WHEN TO USE 1-1 QUESTIONS

Objective:

Child must understand what he/she says has to match the number of words on the page.

Example 1

Child reads: The giraffe has a long neck.
Text reads: The giraffe has a neck. So long!

Strategy

Teacher: "Did your finger match the words?"

Child: "No."

Teacher: "Reread."

If the finger does not match the second time, you take the child's finger and point to the words together.

Example 2

Child reads: The giraffe has a neck it's so long.
Text reads: The giraffe has a neck. So long!

Strategy

Teacher: "Did your finger match the words?"

Child: "No."

Teacher: "Reread."

If the child responds, "Yes, my finger did match," take the child's finger and point to the words together.

LETTER Nn AWARD

When the child has successfully read his/her own *My Nn Book* to you, reward the child with an award. Copy and cut out the one shown here. Pin the award to the child's clothes.

I can read
<u>My Nn Book</u>.
Just ask me!

_____
(name)

<u>CONCLUSION OF LESSON</u>

Remind the child to leave the award on until a grown-up at home asks him/her to read the book.

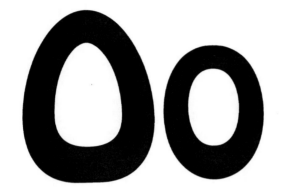

LETTER

Oo

LESSON 1

Objective:

Child will

- visually recognize letter by name.
- recognize the sound /o/ in the initial position by naming words with o in that position.

Materials:

- Large chart with poem, *Oscar the Octopus* (see directions on p. x)
- Any alphabet card with the letter Oo
- Letter Oo can, containing such items as:
  - magazine pictures of octopus, ocean, and owl
  - plastic orange
  - toy octopus

Procedure:

STEP 1

1. Introduce the lesson with the poem, *Oscar the Octopus.*
2. Display the poem on an easel. You read the poem modeling 1-1 match with a pointer.

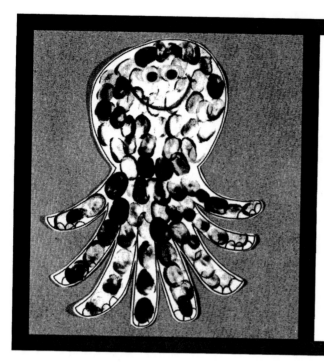

Oscar the Octopus

Oscar the octopus lives deep
in the sea.
Moving about so wild and free.
Swimming and searching to find
a good treat.
With his eight legs reaching
for things he can eat!

3. Ask the whole group, "What letter of the alphabet do you think we are studying now?"
4. Ask children to echo read the poem several times.
5. Ask children for suggestions of movements for acting out the poem.
6. Reread the poem together, acting it out!
7. Put the poem aside.

STEP 2

1. Display the alphabet card with the letter Oo.
2. Ask children to name the letter they see on the alphabet card.
3. Hold up the letter Oo can.
4. Ask children to predict what would make sense in an Oo can.
5. Take each object/picture out of the can. Name them.
6. Ask children to repeat the name of each object/picture after you name it.
7. Show children a sample of the art activity.
8. You now do the art activity with the children, either as a small group or whole class.

ART ACTIVITY

Thumbprint Octopus

Materials:
- Blackline master of poem *Oscar the Octopus*
- Blackline master of Oscar the Octopus
- Green construction paper 12″ × 18″
- Blue tempera paint
- Scissors
- Dish soap
- Wiggly eyes
- Red crayon
- Stapler

Preparation:
Reproduce the poem *Oscar the Octopus* and staple it to the right side of the green construction paper. Mix 1/4 cup of dish soap with 3/4 cup of blue paint.

Procedure:
1. Children trace over the smile with the red crayon.
2. Children dip their thumbs into the paint.
3. With teacher guidance, children press their thumbs on the blackline of the octopus. The octopus should be completely filled in with thumbprints.
4. Let dry.
5. With teacher guidance, children cut out the octopus and glue on wiggly eyes.
6. Staple the octopus to left side of the green construction paper.
7. Send the poem and art activity home. This gives family members an opportunity to reread the poem with the child, reinforcing the letter Oo.

CONCLUSION OF LESSON

Remind children they have learned to recognize letter Oo and they can think of words that have Oo in the initial position.

Oscar the Octopus

Oscar the octopus lives

deep in the sea.

Moving about so wild

and free.

Swimming and searching to

find a good treat.

With his eight legs reaching

for things he can eat!

Oscar the Octopus

Oscar the octopus lives

deep in the sea.

Moving about so wild

and free.

Swimming and searching to

find a good treat.

With his eight legs reaching

for things he can eat!

BLACKLINE MASTER—OSCAR THE OCTOPUS

LESSON 2

Objective:

Children will read *My Oo Book* using 1-1 match.

Materials:

- Big Book—*My Oo Book* (see directions p. xi)
- Large poem—*Oscar the Octopus* (see directions p. x)
- Little books—*My Oo Book* (see directions p. xi)
- Crayons

Procedure:

1. Introduce the lesson with the poem *Oscar the Octopus.*
2. You reread the poem *Oscar the Octopus* modeling 1-1 match with a pointer. Children echo read the poem and act it out.
3. You hold up the "big book," *My Oo Book.* You read the title. Children echo read.
4. You go through each page of the "big book," covering all print. You name the picture on the page. Tell the children to listen for Oo words.
5. You read through the "big book" one time, modeling 1-1 match and directionality.
6. Invite the children to now read the "big book" with you. Model 1-1 match and directionality while reading.
7. The children read through the book a third time while you point to the words.

INDEPENDENT ACTIVITY

1. Reproduce blackline master of the little *My Oo Book.* Give children their own little *My Oo Book* and have them color it in.
2. After children color in their own little *My Oo Book,* they read their book to a partner.
3. You monitor the activity, looking for 1-1 match and directionality.
4. Collect the books.

CONCLUSION OF LESSON

1. You gather the whole group back together for whole group instruction.
2. Everyone rereads the "big book," *My Oo Book,* together.
3. While the children are reading the "big book," you model 1-1 match and directionality, while pointing to the words.

My Oo Book

_____

(name)

- -

Look at the oak tree.

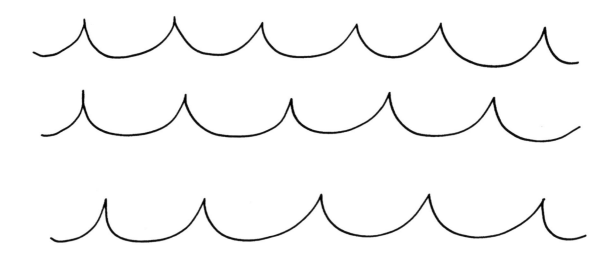

Look at the ocean.

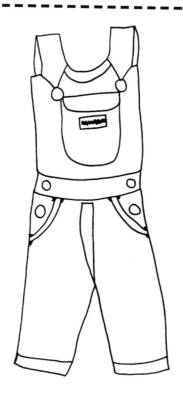

Look at the overalls.

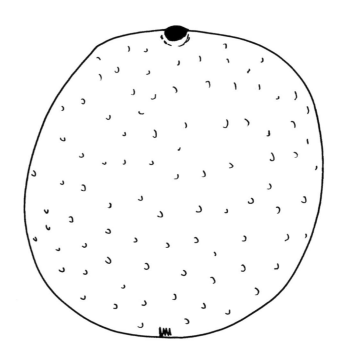

Look at the orange.

Look at the octopus.
Eight legs!

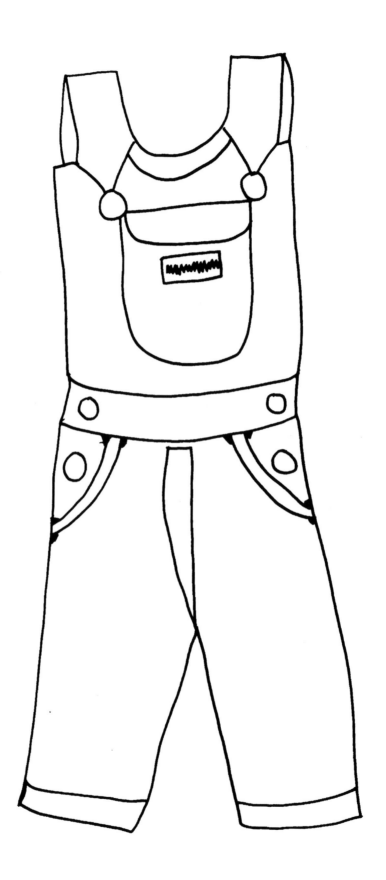

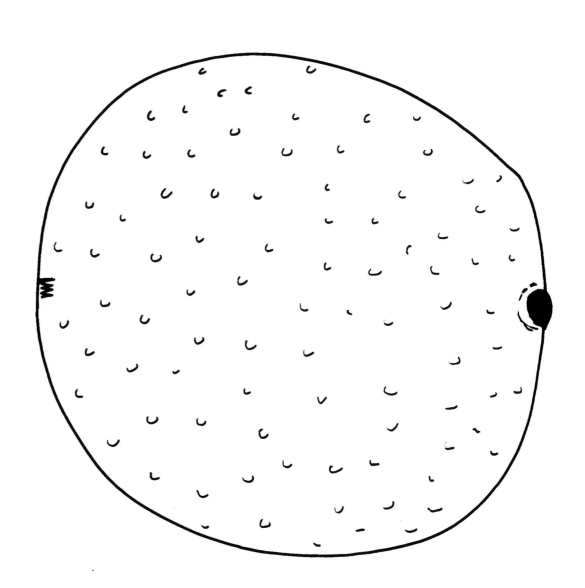

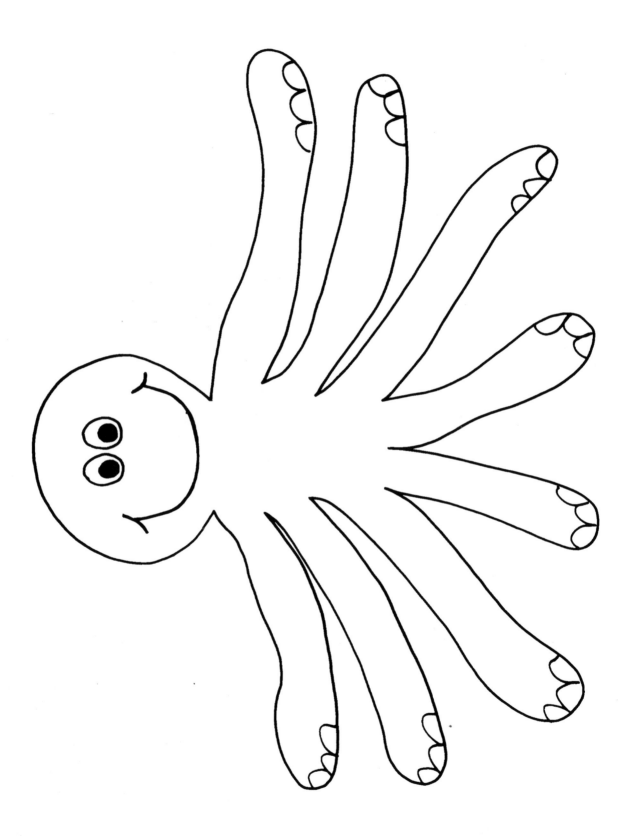

LESSON 3

Objective:

Child will focus on the 4 main cueing systems while reading little book, *My Oo Book.*

Materials:

- Big Book—*My Oo Book*
- Little books—*My Oo Book*
- Awards (see directions p. xii)
- Safety pins

Procedure:

1. Introduce the lesson with the "big book," *My Oo Book.*
2. You read the "big book" with the children, modeling 1-1 match and directionality while pointing to the words.
3. Echo read the book.

INDIVIDUALIZED INSTRUCTION

Note—The objective is to focus the child on the 4 main cueing systems:

- Meaning
- Visual
- Structure
- 1-1 Match

(See page viii for definition and more information.)

1. You now take each child, one at a time, having him/her read the little book, *My Oo Book* to you. Child points to words while reading.
2. As the child is reading to you, you are listening for misread text and prompting the child with the appropriate question to help him/her correct the error. Your phrasing of the questions must be consistent with those in the "Examples of Misread Text."
3. Through repeated use of these techniques, the children will begin to ask themselves these questions. This indicates the child is now monitoring his/her own reading and is on the way to becoming an independent reader.
4. Following are specific examples of misread text by a child using little *My Oo Book.* Find the type of example that matches what your student has read. After using the appropriate strategy questions and the child still can-

not recall the word, then tell the child the word! Teach the child right from the start that reading is *not* a trick!

5. The child's response may not be an exact match to the example. However, if the response is a similar mistake, prompt the child with the appropriate question.

Examples of Misread Text

Following are specific examples of misread text by a child using little *My Oo Book.* Find the type of example that matches what your student has read. Keep in mind that the child's response may not be an exact match to the example. However, if the response is a similar mistake, prompt the child with the appropriate question.

WHEN TO USE MEANING QUESTIONS

Objective:

Child must determine if what he/she has read makes sense in relation to the picture and in the context of the book he/she is reading.

Example

Child reads: Look at the dress.
Text reads: Look at the overalls.

Strategy

Teacher: "Look at the picture. Is that a dress?"

Child: "No. It's overalls."

Teacher: "Good! *Good readers reread.*"

WHEN TO USE STRUCTURE QUESTIONS

Objective:

Child must be able to hear what he/she has read and determine if it sounds right grammatically.

Example

Child reads: Look at orange.
Text reads: Look at the orange.

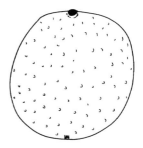

Strategy

Teacher: "Does that sound right? Is that how people talk?"

Child: "No."

Teacher: "What would sound right?"

Child: "Look at the orange."

Teacher: "Good! *Good readers reread.*"

WHEN TO USE VISUAL QUESTIONS

Objective:

Child will use letter in the initial position to read a word in context.

Example

Child reads: Look at the water.
Text reads: Look at the ocean.

Strategy

You point to the misread word: "What word do you know that starts with the letter o and makes sense?"

Child: "Ocean."

Teacher: "Reread."

Child: "Look at the ocean."

If the child hesitates and cannot recall the word, give it! Then have the child reread.

WHEN TO USE 1-1 QUESTIONS

Objective:

Child must understand what he/she says has to match the number of words on the page.

Example 1

Child reads: Look at the tree.
Text reads: Look at the oak tree.

Strategy

Teacher:	"Did your finger match the words?"
Child:	"No."
Teacher:	"Reread."

If the finger does not match the second time, you take the child's finger and point to the words together.

Example 2

Child reads: Look at the octopus with eight legs.
Text reads: Look at the octopus. Eight legs!

Strategy

Teacher:	"Did your finger match the words?"
Child:	"No."
Teacher:	"Reread."

If the child responds, "Yes, my finger did match," take the child's finger and point to the words together.

LETTER Oo AWARD

When the child has successfully read his/her own *My Oo Book* to you, reward the child with an award. Copy and cut out the one shown here. Pin the award to the child's clothes.

I can read
<u>My *Oo* Book</u>.
Just ask me!

_____
(name)

<u>C</u>ONCLUSION OF <u>L</u>ESSON

Remind the child to leave the award on until a grown-up at home asks him/her to read the book.

LETTER

LESSON 1

Objective:

Child will

▪ visually recognize letter by name.
▪ recognize the sound /p/ in the initial position by naming words with p in that position.

Materials:

▪ Large chart with poem, *Polly the Penguin* (see directions on p. x)
▪ Any alphabet card with the letter Pp
▪ Letter Pp can, containing such items as:
  – toy pig
  – peanut in shell
  – paintbrush
  – pencil
  – pen

Procedure:

STEP 1

1. Introduce the lesson with the poem, *Polly the Penguin.*
2. Display the poem on an easel. You read the poem modeling 1-1 match with a pointer.

Polly the Penguin

Polly the penguin
loves to play,
She slips and slides,
everyday.
The arctic is where
penguins live.
Across the ice,
and in the snow.
That's where Polly
likes to go!

3. Ask the whole group, "What letter of the alphabet do you think we are studying now?"
4. Ask children to echo read the poem several times.
5. Ask children for suggestions of movements for acting out the poem.
6. Reread the poem together, acting it out!
7. Put the poem aside.

STEP 2

1. Display the alphabet card with the letter Pp.
2. Ask children to name the letter they see on the alphabet card.
3. Hold up the letter Pp can.
4. Ask children to predict what would make sense in a Pp can.
5. Take each object/picture out of the can. Name them.
6. Ask children to repeat the name of each object/picture after you name it.
7. Show children a sample of the art activity.

8. You now do the art activity with the children, either as a small group or whole class.

ART ACTIVITY

Polly the Penguin

Materials:

- Blackline master of poem *Polly the Penguin*
- Blackline master of Polly the Penguin
- Orange crayons
- Orange construction paper 6" × 9"
- Black watercolor paint
- Watercolor brushes
- Scissors
- Stapler

Preparation:

Reproduce the poem *Polly the Penguin* and staple it to the right side of the orange construction paper.

Procedure:

1. Children paint the penguin using black watercolor paint, leaving feet, beak, and belly white.
2. Children use orange crayon to color beak and feet.
3. Let dry.
4. Cut out the penguin.
5. Staple Polly to left side of the orange construction paper.
6. Send the poem and art activity home. This gives family members an opportunity to reread the poem with the child, reinforcing the letter Pp.

CONCLUSION OF LESSON

Remind children they have learned to recognize letter Pp and they can think of words that have Pp in the initial position.

Polly the Penguin

Polly the penguin,

loves to play.

She slips and slides, everyday.

The arctic is where

penguins live.

Across the ice,

and in the snow,

That's where Polly

likes to go!

Polly the Penguin

Polly the penguin,

loves to play.

She slips and slides, everyday.

The arctic is where

penguins live.

Across the ice,

and in the snow,

That's where Polly

likes to go!

BLACKLINE MASTER—POEM

BLACKLINE MASTER—POLLY THE PENGUIN

LESSON 2

Objective:

Children will read *My Pp Book* using 1-1 match.

Materials:

- Big Book—*My Pp Book* (see directions p. xi)
- Large poem—*Polly the Penguin* (see directions p. x)
- Little books—*My Pp Book* (see directions p. xi)
- Crayons

Procedure:

1. Introduce the lesson with the poem *Polly the Penguin.*
2. You reread the poem *Polly the Penguin* modeling 1-1 match with a pointer. Children echo read the poem and act it out.
3. You hold up the "big book," *My Pp Book.* You read the title. Children echo read.
4. You go through each page of the "big book," covering all print. You name the picture on the page. Tell the children to listen for Pp words.
5. You read through the "big book" one time, modeling 1-1 match and directionality.
6. Invite the children to now read the "big book" with you. Model 1-1 match and directionality while reading.
7. The children read through the book a third time while you point to the words.

INDEPENDENT ACTIVITY

1. Reproduce blackline master of the little *My Pp Book.* Give children their own little *My Pp Book* and have them color it in.
2. After children color in their own little *My Pp Book,* they read their book to a partner.
3. You monitor the activity, looking for 1-1 match and directionality.
4. Collect the books.

CONCLUSION OF LESSON

1. You gather the whole group back together for whole group instruction.
2. Everyone rereads the "big book," *My Pp Book,* together.
3. While the children are reading the "big book," you model 1-1 match and directionality, while pointing to the words.

My Pp Book

_____

(name)

The pony can run.

The pig can run.

The penguin can run.

The peacock can run.

The puppy can run to me!

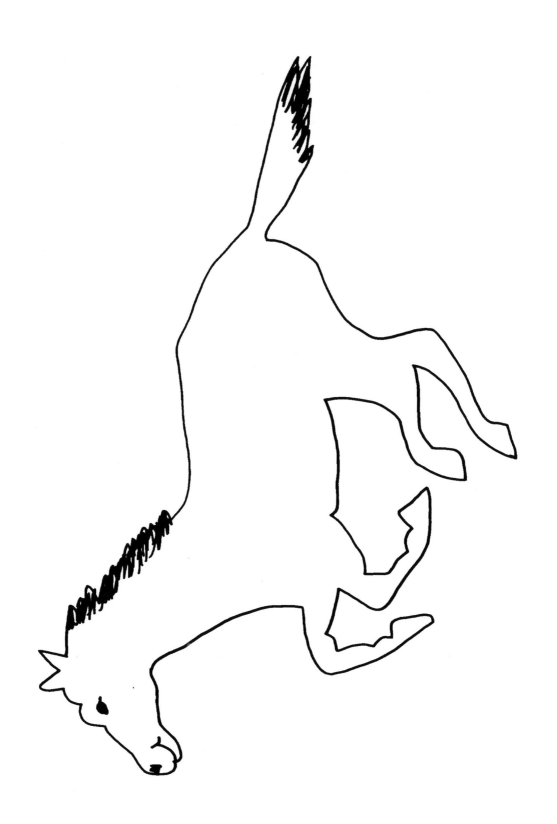

LESSON 3

Objective:

Child will focus on the 4 main cueing systems while reading little book, *My Pp Book.*

Materials:

▮ Big Book—*My Pp Book*
▮ Little books—*My Pp Book*
▮ Awards (see directions p. xii)
▮ Safety pins

Procedure:

1. Introduce the lesson with the "big book," *My Pp Book.*
2. You read the "big book" with the children, modeling 1-1 match and directionality while pointing to the words.
3. Echo read the book.

INDIVIDUALIZED INSTRUCTION

Note—The objective is to focus the child on the 4 main cueing systems:

▮ Meaning
▮ Visual
▮ Structure
▮ 1-1 Match

(See page viii for definition and more information.)

1. You now take each child, one at a time, having him/her read the little book, *My Pp Book,* to you. Child points to words while reading.
2. As the child is reading to you, you are listening for misread text and prompting the child with the appropriate question to help him/her correct the error. Your phrasing of the questions must be consistent with those in the "Examples of Misread Text."
3. Through repeated use of these techniques, the children will begin to ask themselves these questions. This indicates the child is now monitoring his/her own reading and is on the way to becoming an independent reader.
4. Following are specific examples of misread text by a child using little *My Pp Book.* Find the type of example that matches what your student has read. After using the appropriate strategy questions and the child still

cannot recall the word, then tell the child the word! Teach the child right from the start that reading is *not* a trick!

5. The child's response may not be an exact match to the example. However, if the response is a similar mistake, prompt the child with the appropriate question.

Examples of Misread Text

Following are specific examples of misread text by a child using little *My Pp Book.* Find the type of example that matches what your student has read. Keep in mind that the child's response may not be an exact match to the example. However, if the response is a similar mistake, prompt the child with the appropriate question.

WHEN TO USE MEANING QUESTIONS

Objective:

Child must determine if what he/she has read makes sense in relation to the picture and in the context of the book he/she is reading.

Example

Child reads:	The bird can run.
Text reads:	The penguin can run.

Strategy

Teacher:	"Does bird make sense in a Pp book?"
Child:	"No."
Teacher:	"What else could you try?"
Child:	"Penguin."
Teacher:	"Good! Penguin begins with p. *Good readers reread.*"

WHEN TO USE STRUCTURE QUESTIONS

Objective:

Child must be able to hear what he/she has read and determine if it sounds right grammatically.

Example

Child reads: The pig is run.
Text reads: The pig can run.

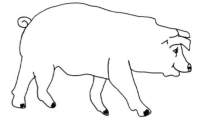

Strategy

Teacher: "Does that sound right? Is that how people talk?"

Child: "No."

Teacher: "What would sound right?"

Child: "The pig can run."

Teacher: "Good! *Good readers reread.*"

WHEN TO USE VISUAL QUESTIONS

Objective:

Child will use letter in the initial position to read a word in context.

Example

Child reads: The horse can run.
Text reads: The pony can run.

Strategy

You point to the misread word: "What sound does the letter p make?"

Child: "Pppp."

Teacher: "Reread."

Child: "The pony can run."

If the child hesitates and cannot recall the word, give it! Then have the child reread.

WHEN TO USE 1-1 QUESTIONS

Objective:

Child must understand what he/she says has to match the number of words on the page.

Example 1

Child reads: The puppy run to me.
Text reads: The puppy can run to me!

Strategy

Teacher: "Did your finger match the words?"

Child: "No."

Teacher: "Reread."

If the finger does not match the second time, you take the child's finger and point to the words together.

Example 2

Child reads: The pony can run fast.
Text reads: The pony can run.

Strategy

Teacher: "Did your finger match the words?"

Child: "No."

Teacher: "Reread."

If the child responds, "Yes, my finger did match," take the child's finger and point to the words together.

LETTER Pp AWARD

When the child has successfully read his/her own *My Pp Book* to you, reward the child with an award. Copy and cut out the one shown here. Pin the award to the child's clothes.

I can read
My Pp Book.
Just ask me!

_____
(name)

<u>CONCLUSION OF LESSON</u>

Remind the child to leave the award on until a grown-up at home asks him/her to read the book.

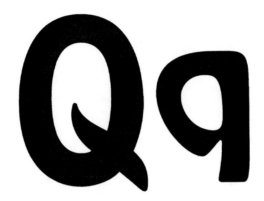

LESSON 1

Objective:

Child will

∎ visually recognize letter by name.

∎ recognize the sound /q/ in the initial position by naming words with q in that position.

Materials:

∎ Large chart with poem, *A Quilt* (see directions on p. x)

∎ Any alphabet card with the letter Qq

∎ Letter Qq can, containing such items as:
  – magazine pictures of a quilt and of a queen
  – quarter
  – question mark (use a permanent marker to draw a ? on an unlined 3″ × 5″ card

Procedure:

STEP 1

1. Introduce the lesson with the poem, *A Quilt.*

2. Display the poem on an easel. You read the poem modeling 1-1 match with a pointer.

A Quilt

A quilt is like a blanket,
It keeps you nice and warm.
You pull it up around your chin,
When your parents,
tuck you in.
Soft and cozy,
Colorful and bright.
It keeps you feeling,
safe at night.

3. Ask the whole group, "What letter of the alphabet do you think we are studying now?"
4. Ask children to echo read the poem several times.
5. Ask children for suggestions of movements for acting out the poem.
6. Reread the poem together, acting it out!
7. Put the poem aside.

STEP 2

1. Display the alphabet card with the letter Qq.
2. Ask children to name the letter they see on the alphabet card.
3. Hold up the letter Qq can.
4. Ask children to predict what would make sense in a Qq can.
5. Take each object/picture out of the can. Name them.

6. Ask children to repeat the name of each object/picture after you name it.
7. Show children a sample of the art activity.
8. You now do the art activity with the children, either as a small group or whole class.

ART ACTIVITY

Colorful Quilt

Materials:
- Blackline master of poem *A Quilt*
- Blackline master of quilt
- Colored markers
- Pink construction paper 12″ × 18″
- Stapler

Preparation:
Reproduce the poem *A Quilt* and staple it to the right side of the pink construction paper.

Procedure:
1. Children color in designs on the quilt with the markers.
2. Staple quilt to left side of the pink construction paper.
3. Send the poem and art activity home. This gives family members an opportunity to reread the poem with the child, reinforcing the letter Qq.

CONCLUSION OF LESSON

Remind children they have learned to recognize letter Qq and they can think of words that have Qq in the initial position.

A Quilt

A quilt is like a blanket,

It keeps you nice and warm.

You pull it up around your

chin, when your parents

   tuck you in.

Soft and cozy, colorful and

bright. It keeps you feeling,

   safe at night.

- -

A Quilt

A quilt is like a blanket,

It keeps you nice and warm.

You pull it up around your

chin, when your parents

   tuck you in.

Soft and cozy, colorful and

bright. It keeps you feeling,

   safe at night.

BLACKLINE MASTER—POEM

LESSON 2

Objective:

Children will read *My Qq Book* using 1-1 match.

Materials:

- Big Book—*My Qq Book* (see directions p. xi)
- Large poem—*A Quilt* (see directions p. x)
- Little books—*My Qq Book* (see directions p. xi)
- Crayons

Procedure:

1. Introduce the lesson with the poem *A Quilt*.
2. You reread the poem *A Quilt* modeling 1-1 match with a pointer. Children echo read the poem and act it out.
3. You hold up the "big book," *My Qq Book*. You read the title. Children echo read.
4. You go through each page of the "big book," covering all print. You name the picture on the page. Tell the children to listen for Qq words.
5. You read through the "big book" one time, modeling 1-1 match and directionality.
6. Invite the children to now read the "big book" with you. Model 1-1 match and directionality while reading.
7. The children read through the book a third time while you point to the words.

INDEPENDENT ACTIVITY

1. Reproduce blackline master of the little *My Qq Book*. Give children their own little *My Qq Book* and have them color it in.
2. After children color in their own little *My Qq Book*, they read their book to a partner.
3. You monitor the activity, looking for 1-1 match and directionality.
4. Collect the books.

CONCLUSION OF LESSON

1. You gather the whole group back together for whole group instruction.
2. Everyone rereads the "big book," *My Qq Book*, together.
3. While the children are reading the "big book," you model 1-1 match and directionality, while pointing to the words.

My Qq Book

_____

- -

Here is a queen.

Here is a quarter.

- -

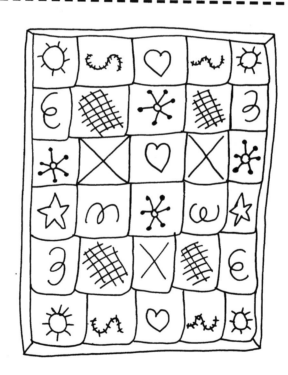

Here is a quilt.

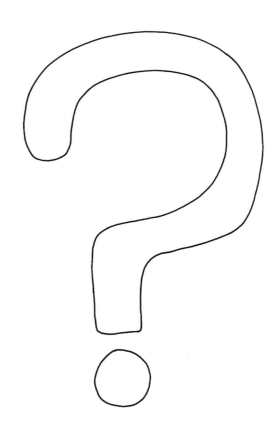

Here is a question mark.
See it?

F

LESSON 3

Objective:

Child will focus on the 4 main cueing systems while reading little book, *My Qq Book.*

Materials:

- Big Book—*My Qq Book*
- Little books—*My Qq Book*
- Awards (see directions p. xii)
- Safety pins

Procedure:

1. Introduce the lesson with the "big book," *My Qq Book.*
2. You read the "big book" with the children, modeling 1-1 match and directionality while pointing to the words.
3. Echo read the book.

INDIVIDUALIZED INSTRUCTION

Note—The objective is to focus the child on the 4 main cueing systems:

- Meaning
- Visual
- Structure
- 1-1 Match

(See page viii for definition and more information.)

1. You now take each child, one at a time, having him/her read the little book, *My Qq Book* to you. Child points to words while reading.
2. As the child is reading to you, you are listening for misread text and prompting the child with the appropriate question to help him/her correct the error. Your phrasing of the questions must be consistent with those in the "Examples of Misread Text."
3. Through repeated use of these techniques, the children will begin to ask themselves these questions. This indicates the child is now monitoring his/her own reading and is on the way to becoming an independent reader.
4. Following are specific examples of misread text by a child using little *My Qq Book.* Find the type of example that matches what your student has

read. After using the appropriate strategy questions and the child still cannot recall the word, then tell the child the word! Teach the child right from the start that reading is *not* a trick!

5. The child's response may not be an exact match to the example. However, if the response is a similar mistake, prompt the child with the appropriate question.

Examples of Misread Text

Following are specific examples of misread text by a child using little *My Qq Book*. Find the type of example that matches what your student has read. Keep in mind that the child's response may not be an exact match to the example. However, if the response is a similar mistake, prompt the child with the appropriate question.

WHEN TO USE MEANING QUESTIONS

Objective:

Child must determine if what he/she has read makes sense in relation to the picture and in the context of the book he/she is reading.

Example

Child reads: Here is a lady.
Text reads: Here is a queen.

Strategy

Teacher: "Look at the picture. Is that an ordinary lady?"

Child: "No. It's a queen."

Teacher: "Good! *Good readers reread.*"

WHEN TO USE STRUCTURE QUESTIONS

Objective:

Child must be able to hear what he/she has read and determine if it sounds right grammatically.

Example

Child reads: Here a quarter.
Text reads: Here is a quarter.

Strategy

Teacher: "Does that sound right? Is that how people talk?"

Child: "No."

Teacher: "What would sound right?"

Child: "Here is a quarter."

Teacher: "Good! *Good readers reread.*"

WHEN TO USE VISUAL QUESTIONS

Objective:

Child will use letter in the initial position to read a word in context.

Example

Child reads: Here is a blanket.
Text reads: Here is a quilt.

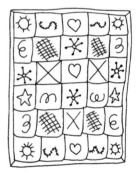

Strategy

You point to the misread word: "What word do you know that starts with letter q and makes sense?"

Child: "Quilt."

Teacher: "Reread."

Child: "Here is a quilt."

If the child hesitates and cannot recall the word, give it! Then have the child reread.

WHEN TO USE 1-1 QUESTIONS

Objective:

Child must understand what he/she says has to match the number of words on the page.

Example 1

Child reads: Here is a question mark.
Text reads: Here is a question mark. See it?

Strategy

Teacher: "Did your finger match the words?"

Child: "No."

Teacher: "Reread."

If the finger does not match the second time, you take the child's finger and point to the words together.

Example 2

Child reads: Here is a pretty queen.
Text reads: Here is a queen.

Strategy

Teacher: · "Did your finger match the words?"

Child: "No."

Teacher: "Reread."

If the child responds, "Yes, my finger did match," take the child's finger and point to the words together.

LETTER Qq AWARD

When the child has successfully read his/her own *My Qq Book* to you, reward the child with an award. Copy and cut out the one shown here. Pin the award to the child's clothes.

CONCLUSION OF LESSON

Remind the child to leave the award on until a grown-up at home asks him/her to read the book.

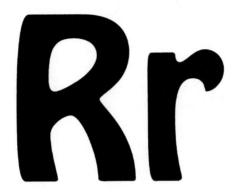

LESSON 1

Objective:

Child will

■ visually recognize letter by name.

■ recognize the sound /r/ in the initial position by naming words with r in that position.

Materials:

■ Large chart with poem, *Little Rabbit* (see directions on p. x)

■ Any alphabet card with the letter Rr

■ Letter Rr can, containing such items as:
   - magazine pictures of a raccoon and of a rainbow
   - toy ring
   - toy rabbit
   - ribbon
   - small piece of *red* paper

Procedure:

STEP 1

1. Introduce the lesson with the poem, *Little Rabbit.*
2. Display the poem on an easel. You read the poem modeling 1-1 match with a pointer.

Little Rabbit

I know a little rabbit,
that goes hop, hop, hop.
When I try to catch him,
I say "Stop, stop, stop."
He often tries to hide from me,
Jumping in his hole and out.
"Come back Little Rabbit!"
I often have to shout.

3. Ask the whole group, "What letter of the alphabet do you think we are studying now?"
4. Ask children to echo read the poem several times.
5. Ask children for suggestions of movements for acting out the poem.
6. Reread the poem together, acting it out!
7. Put the poem aside.

STEP 2

1. Display the alphabet card with the letter Rr.
2. Ask children to name the letter they see on the alphabet card.
3. Hold up the letter Rr can.
4. Ask children to predict what would make sense in an Rr can.
5. Take each object/picture out of the can. Name them.
6. Ask children to repeat the name of each object/picture after you name it.
7. Show children a sample of the art activity.

8. You now do the art activity with the children, either as a small group or whole class.

ART ACTIVITY

Rockin' Rabbit

Materials:

- Blackline master of poem *Little Rabbit*
- Blackline master of rabbit
- Crayons
- Green construction paper 12" × 18"
- 2 - 12" long pipe cleaners per child (any color)
- Scissors
- Stapler

Preparation:

Reproduce the poem *Little Rabbit* and staple it to the right side of the green construction paper.

Procedure:

1. Children color the rabbit with the gray crayon, leaving the inside of the ears and nose white.
2. Children use pink crayons to color inside the ears and the nose.
3. Children cut out the rabbit.
4. With teacher guidance, children push pipe cleaners through the right side of the nose and out the left side of the nose to create whiskers.
5. Staple rabbit to left side of the green construction paper.
6. Send the poem and art activity home. This gives family members an opportunity to reread the poem with the child, reinforcing the letter Rr.

CONCLUSION OF LESSON

Remind children they have learned to recognize letter Rr and they can think of words that have Rr in the initial position.

Little Rabbit

I know a little rabbit that goes

hop, hop, hop.

When I try to catch him, I say,

"Stop, stop, stop."

He often tries to hide from me,

jumping in his hole and out.

"Come back, Little Rabbit!" I

often have to shout.

Little Rabbit

I know a little rabbit that goes

hop, hop, hop.

When I try to catch him, I say,

"Stop, stop, stop."

He often tries to hide from me,

jumping in his hole and out.

"Come back, Little Rabbit!" I

often have to shout.

BLACKLINE MASTER—POEM

BLACKLINE MASTER—LITTLE RABBIT

LESSON 2

Objective:

Children will read *My Rr Book* using 1-1 match.

Materials:

■ Big Book—*My Rr Book* (see directions p. xi)
■ Large poem—*Little Rabbit* (see directions p. x)
■ Little books—*My Rr Book* (see directions p. xi)
■ Crayons

Procedure:

1. Introduce the lesson with the poem *Little Rabbit.*
2. You reread the poem *Little Rabbit* modeling 1-1 match with a pointer. Children echo read the poem and act it out.
3. You hold up the "big book," *My Rr Book.* You read the title. Children echo read.
4. You go through each page of the "big book," covering all print. You name the picture on the page. Tell the children to listen for Rr words.
5. You read through the "big book" one time, modeling 1-1 match and directionality.
6. Invite the children to now read the "big book" with you. Model 1-1 match and directionality while reading.
7. The children read through the book a third time while you point to the words.

INDEPENDENT ACTIVITY

1. Reproduce blackline master of the little *My Rr Book.* Give children their own little *My Rr Book* and have them color it in.
2. After children color in their own little *My Rr Book,* they read their book to a partner.
3. You monitor the activity, looking for 1-1 match and directionality.
4. Collect the books.

CONCLUSION OF LESSON

1. You gather the whole group back together for whole group instruction.
2. Everyone rereads the "big book," *My Rr Book,* together.
3. While the children are reading the "big book," you model 1-1 match and directionality, while pointing to the words.

My Rr Book

_____

(name)

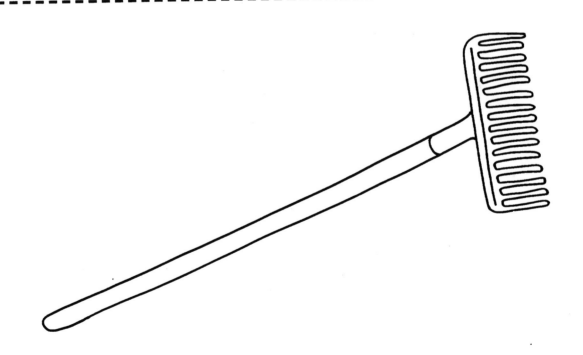

Here is a rake.

Here is a rabbit.

- -

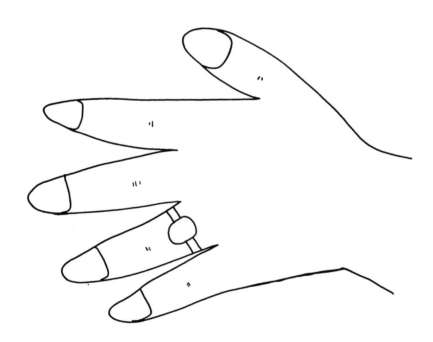

Here is a ring.

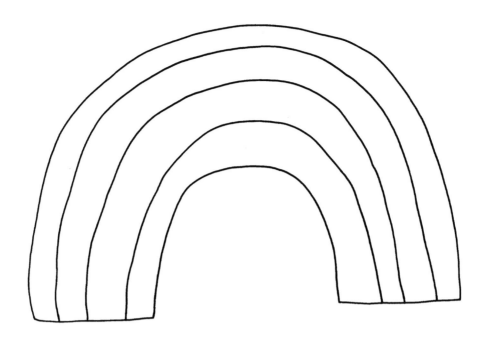

Here is a rainbow.

Here is a rooster.
Cock-a-doodle-doo!

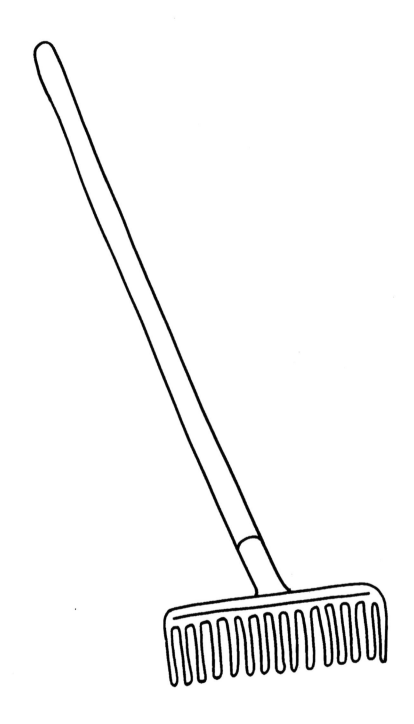

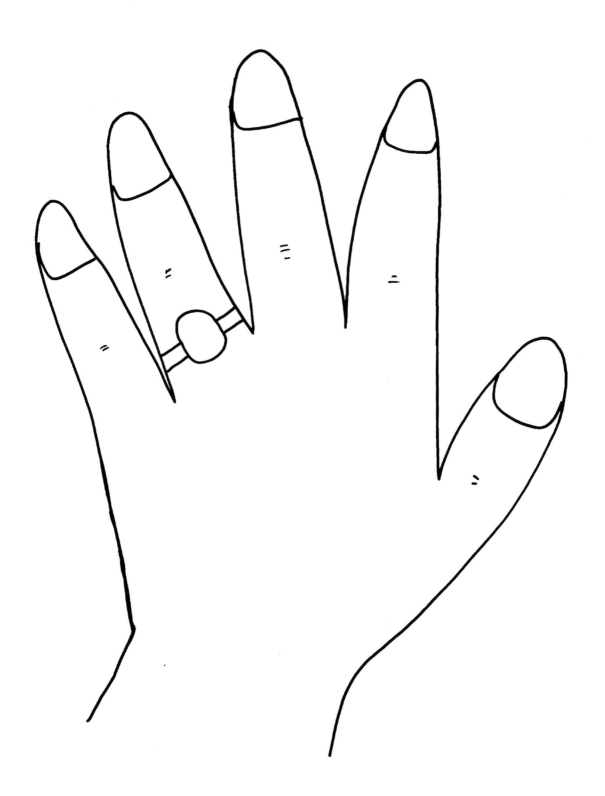

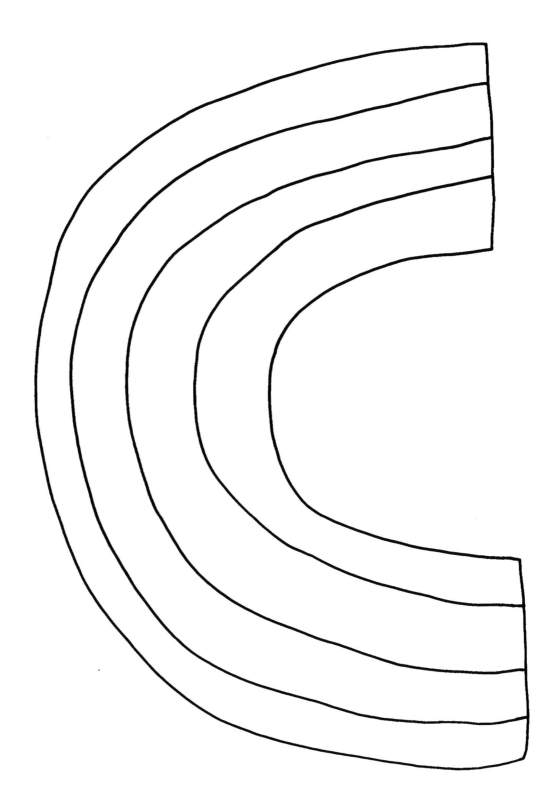

F

LESSON 3

Objective:

Child will focus on the 4 main cueing systems while reading little book, *My Rr Book.*

Materials:

▪ Big Book—*My Rr Book*
▪ Little books—*My Rr Book*
▪ Awards (see directions p. xii)
▪ Safety pins

Procedure:

1. Introduce the lesson with the "big book," *My Rr Book.*
2. You read the "big book" with the children, modeling 1-1 match and directionality while pointing to the words.
3. Echo read the book.

INDIVIDUALIZED INSTRUCTION

Note—The objective is to focus the child on the 4 main cueing systems:

▪ Meaning
▪ Visual
▪ Structure
▪ 1-1 Match

(See page viii for definition and more information.)

1. You now take each child, one at a time, having him/her read the little book, *My Rr Book,* to you. Child points to words while reading.
2. As the child is reading to you, you are listening for misread text and prompting the child with the appropriate question to help him/her correct the error. Your phrasing of the questions must be consistent with those in the "Examples of Misread Text."
3. Through repeated use of these techniques, the children will begin to ask themselves these questions. This indicates the child is now monitoring his/her own reading and is on the way to becoming an independent reader.
4. Following are specific examples of misread text by a child using little *My Rr Book.* Find the type of example that matches what your student has read. After using the appropriate strategy questions and the child still

cannot recall the word, then tell the child the word! Teach the child right from the start that reading is *not* a trick!

5. The child's response may not be an exact match to the example. However, if the response is a similar mistake, prompt the child with the appropriate question.

Examples of Misread Text

Following are specific examples of misread text by a child using little *My Rr Book*. Find the type of example that matches what your student has read. Keep in mind that the child's response may not be an exact match to the example. However, if the response is a similar mistake, prompt the child with the appropriate question.

WHEN TO USE MEANING QUESTIONS

Objective:

Child must determine if what he/she has read makes sense in relation to the picture and in the context of the book he/she is reading.

Example

Child reads:	Here is a chicken.
Text reads:	Here is a rooster. Cock-a-doodle-doo!

Strategy

Teacher:	"Does chicken make sense in an Rr book?"
Child:	"No."
Teacher:	"What else could you try?"
Child:	"Rooster."
Teacher:	"Good! Rooster begins with r. *Good readers reread.*"

WHEN TO USE STRUCTURE QUESTIONS

Objective:

Child must be able to hear what he/she has read and determine if it sounds right grammatically.

Letter Rr

Example

Child reads: Here a rake.
Text reads: Here is a rake.

Strategy

Teacher: "Does that sound right? Is that how people talk?"

Child: "No."

Teacher: "What would sound right?"

Child: "Here is a rake."

Teacher: "Good! *Good readers reread.*"

WHEN TO USE VISUAL QUESTIONS

Objective:

Child will use letter in the initial position to read a word in context.

Example

Child reads: Here is a bunny.
Text reads: Here is a rabbit.

Strategy

You point to the misread word: "What sound does the letter r make?"

Child: "Rrrr."

Teacher: "Reread."

Child: "Here is a rabbit."

If the child hesitates and cannot recall the word, give it! Then have the child reread.

WHEN TO USE 1-1 QUESTIONS

Objective:

Child must understand what he/she says has to match the number of words on the page.

Example 1

Child reads: Here is a bunny rabbit.
Text reads: Here is a rabbit.

Strategy

Teacher: "Did your finger match the words?"

Child: "No."

Teacher: "Reread."

If the finger does not match the second time, you take the child's finger and point to the words together.

Example 2

Child reads: Here's a ring.
Text reads: Here is a ring.

Strategy

Teacher: "Did your finger match the words?"

Child: "No."

Teacher: "Reread."

If the child responds, "Yes, my finger did match," take the child's finger and point to the words together.

LETTER Rr AWARD

When the child has successfully read his/her own *My Rr Book* to you, reward the child with an award. Copy and cut out the one shown here. Pin the award to the child's clothes.

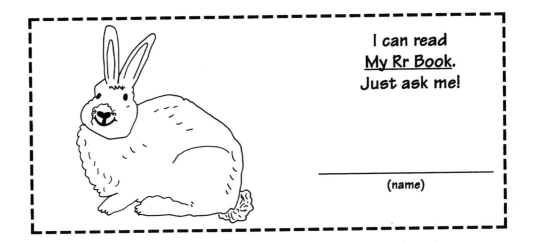

I can read
<u>My Rr Book</u>.
Just ask me!

_____
(name)

CONCLUSION OF LESSON

Remind the child to leave the award on until a grown-up at home asks him/her to read the book.

Ss

LESSON 1

Objective:

Child will

- visually recognize letter by name.
- recognize the sound /s/ in the initial position by naming words with s in that position.

Materials:

- Large chart with poem, *Starfish* (see directions on p. x)
- Any alphabet card with the letter Ss
- Letter Ss can, containing such items as:
  - sock .
  - sneaker (child's)
  - spoon
  - rubber snake
  - starfish

Procedure:

STEP 1

1. Introduce the lesson with the poem, *Starfish.*
2. Display the poem on an easel. You read the poem modeling 1-1 match with a pointer.

Starfish

A starfish is an animal,
that lives in the sea.
It's skin may be smooth or prickly.
Some have five arms,
some have more.
They creep very slowly, on the
ocean floor.
With his arms outstretched
helping him glide,
Looking for food or a place to hide.

3. Ask the whole group, "What letter of the alphabet do you think we are studying now?"
4. Ask children to echo read the poem several times.
5. Ask children for suggestions of movements for acting out the poem.
6. Reread the poem together, acting it out!
7. Put the poem aside.

STEP 2

1. Display the alphabet card with the letter Ss.
2. Ask children to name the letter they see on the alphabet card.
3. Hold up the letter Ss can.
4. Ask children to predict what would make sense in an Ss can.
5. Take each object/picture out of the can. Name them.
6. Ask children to repeat the name of each object/picture after you name it.
7. Show children a sample of the art activity.

8. You now do the art activity with the children, either as a small group or whole class.

ART ACTIVITY

Super Starfish

Materials:

- Blackline master of poem *Starfish*
- Blackline master of starfish
- Watercolors
- Black paint
- Light blue construction paper 6" × 9"
- Q-tips
- Stapler

Preparation:

Reproduce the poem *Starfish* and staple it to the right side of the light blue construction paper.

Procedure:

1. Children paint the starfish using watercolors.
2. Let dry.
3. With teacher guidance, children dip Q-tips into black paint and dab on "bumps."
4. Let dry.
5. Cut out.
6. Staple starfish to left side of the light blue construction paper.
7. Send the poem and art activity home. This gives family members an opportunity to reread the poem with the child, reinforcing the letter Ss.

CONCLUSION OF LESSON

Remind children they have learned to recognize letter Ss and they can think of words that have Ss in the initial position.

Starfish

A starfish is an animal, that

lives in the sea.

It's skin may be smooth,

or prickly. Some have five

arms, some have more.

They creep very slowly, on the

ocean floor. With his arms

outstretched helping him

glide, looking for food,

or a place to hide!

Starfish

A starfish is an animal, that

lives in the sea.

It's skin may be smooth,

or prickly. Some have five

arms, some have more.

They creep very slowly, on the

ocean floor. With his arms out-

stretched helping him glide,

looking for food,

or a place to hide!

©1995 by Roberta Seckler Brown and Susan Carey

BLACKLINE MASTER—POEM

LESSON 2

Objective:

Children will read *My Ss Book* using 1-1 match.

Materials:

- Big Book—*My Ss Book* (see directions p. xi)
- Large poem—*Starfish* (see directions p. x)
- Little books—*My Ss Book* (see directions p. xi)
- Crayons

Procedure:

1. Introduce the lesson with the poem *Starfish.*
2. You reread the poem *Starfish* modeling 1-1 match with a pointer. Children echo read the poem and act it out.
3. You hold up the "big book," *My Ss Book.* You read the title. Children echo read.
4. You go through each page of the "big book," covering all print. You name the picture on the page. Tell the children to listen for Ss words.
5. You read through the "big book" one time, modeling 1-1 match and directionality.
6. Invite the children to now read the "big book" with you. Model 1-1 match and directionality while reading.
7. The children read through the book a third time while you point to the words.

INDEPENDENT ACTIVITY

1. Reproduce blackline master of the little *My Ss Book.* Give children their own little *My Ss Book* and have them color it in.
2. After children color in their own little *My Ss Book,* they read their book to a partner.
3. You monitor the activity, looking for 1-1 match and directionality.
4. Collect the books.

CONCLUSION OF LESSON

1. You gather the whole group back together for whole group instruction.
2. Everyone rereads the "big book," *My Ss Book,* together.
3. While the children are reading the "big book," you model 1-1 match and directionality, while pointing to the words.

My Ss Book

_____

(name)

- -

This is a sign.

This is a snowman.

This is a sock.

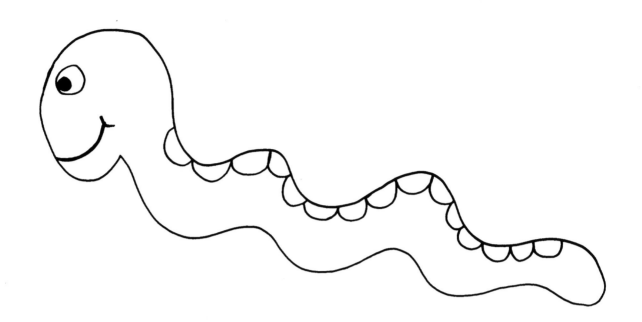

This is a snake.

- -

This is a star. Make a wish!

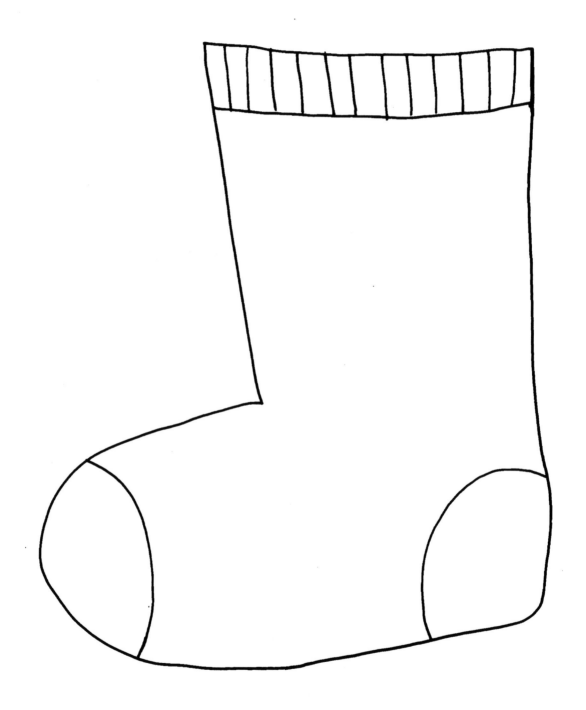

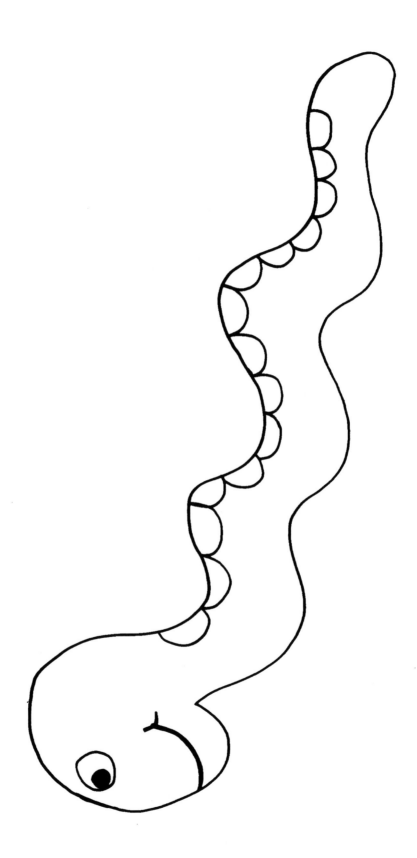

F

LESSON 3

Objective:

Child will focus on the 4 main cueing systems while reading little book, *My Ss Book.*

Materials:

▮ Big Book—*My Ss Book*
▮ Little books—*My Ss Book*
▮ Awards (see directions p. xii)
▮ Safety pins

Procedure:

1. Introduce the lesson with the "big book," *My Ss Book.*
2. You read the "big book" with the children, modeling 1-1 match and directionality while pointing to the words.
3. Echo read the book.

INDIVIDUALIZED INSTRUCTION

Note—The objective is to focus the child on the 4 main cueing systems:

▮ Meaning
▮ Visual
▮ Structure
▮ 1-1 Match

(See page viii for definition and more information.)

1. You now take each child, one at a time, having him/her read the little book, *My Ss Book,* to you. Child points to words while reading.
2. As the child is reading to you, you are listening for misread text and prompting the child with the appropriate question to help him/her correct the error. Your phrasing of the questions must be consistent with those in the "Examples of Misread Text."
3. Through repeated use of these techniques, the children will begin to ask themselves these questions. This indicates the child is now monitoring his/her own reading and is on the way to becoming an independent reader.
4. Following are specific examples of misread text by a child using little *My Ss Book.* Find the type of example that matches what your student has read. After using the appropriate strategy questions and the child still

cannot recall the word, then tell the child the word! Teach the child right from the start that reading is *not* a trick!

5. The child's response may not be an exact match to the example. However, if the response is a similar mistake, prompt the child with the appropriate question.

Examples of Misread Text

Following are specific examples of misread text by a child using little *My Ss Book.* Find the type of example that matches what your student has read. Keep in mind that the child's response may not be an exact match to the example. However, if the response is a similar mistake, prompt the child with the appropriate question.

WHEN TO USE MEANING QUESTIONS

Objective:

Child must determine if what he/she has read makes sense in relation to the picture and in the context of the book he/she is reading.

Example

Child reads: This is a slipper.
Text reads: This is a sock.

Strategy

Teacher: "Look at the picture. Is that a slipper?"

Child: "No. It's a sock."

Teacher: "Good! *Good readers reread.*"

WHEN TO USE STRUCTURE QUESTIONS

Objective:

Child must be able to hear what he/she has read and determine if it sounds right grammatically.

Example

Child reads: Then is a snowman.
Text reads: This is a snowman.

Strategy

Teacher: "Does that sound right? Is that how people talk?"

Child: "No."

Teacher: "What would sound right?"

Child: "This is a snowman."

Teacher: "Good! *Good readers reread."*

WHEN TO USE VISUAL QUESTIONS

Objective:

Child will use letter in the initial position to read a word in context.

Example

Child reads: This is a worm.
Text reads: This is a snake.

Strategy

You point to the misread word: "What sound does the letter s make?"

Child: "Ssss."

Teacher: "Reread."

Child: "This is a snake."

If the child hesitates and cannot recall the word, give it! Then have the child reread.

WHEN TO USE 1-1 QUESTIONS

Objective:

Child must understand what he/she says has to match the number of words on the page.

Example 1

Child reads: This is a stop sign.
Text reads: This is a sign.

Strategy

Teacher: "Did your finger match the words?"

Child: "No."

Teacher: "Reread."

If the finger does not match the second time, you take the child's finger and point to the words together.

Example 2

Child reads: This is a star.
Text reads: This is a star. Make a wish!

Strategy

Teacher: "Did your finger match the words?"

Child: "No."

Teacher: "Reread."

If the child responds, "Yes, my finger did match," take the child's finger and point to the words together.

LETTER Ss AWARD

When the child has successfully read his/her own *My Ss Book* to you, reward the child with an award. Copy and cut out the one shown here. Pin the award to the child's clothes.

I can read
<u>My Ss Book</u>.
Just ask me!

_____
(name)

<u>CONCLUSION OF LESSON</u>

Remind the child to leave the award on until a grown-up at home asks him/her to read the book.

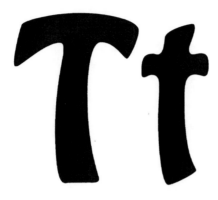

L
E
T
T
E
R

LESSON 1

Objective:

Child will

▮ visually recognize letter by name.

▮ recognize the sound /t/ in the initial position by naming words with t in that position.

Materials:

▮ Large chart with poem, *My Teddy Bear* (see directions on p. x)

▮ Any alphabet card with the letter Tt

▮ Letter Tt can, containing such items as:
  – tongue depressor
  – toothbrush
  – small toothpaste
  – small teddy bear
  – plastic turtle

Procedure:

STEP 1

1. Introduce the lesson with the poem, *My Teddy Bear.*
2. Display the poem on an easel. You read the poem modeling 1-1 match with a pointer.

My Teddy Bear

I have a little teddy bear,
Whose fur is soft and brown.
When I go to sleep at night,
he helps me settle down.
I take him everyplace I go.
My special friend,
I love him so!

3. Ask the whole group, "What letter of the alphabet do you think we are studying now?"
4. Ask children to echo read the poem several times.
5. Ask children for suggestions of movements for acting out the poem.
6. Reread the poem together, acting it out!
7. Put the poem aside.

STEP 2

1. Display the alphabet card with the letter Tt.
2. Ask children to name the letter they see on the alphabet card.
3. Hold up the letter Tt can.
4. Ask children to predict what would make sense in a Tt can.
5. Take each object/picture out of the can. Name them.
6. Ask children to repeat the name of each object/picture after you name it.
7. Show children a sample of the art activity.
8. You now do the art activity with the children, either as a small group or whole class.

ART ACTIVITY

Teddy Bear

Materials:

- Blackline master of poem *My Teddy Bear*
- Blackline master of teddy bear
- Brown and red crayons
- White construction paper 12″ × 18″
- 3 buttons per child
- Wiggly eyes
- 1 colored pompon per child
- Glue
- Scissors
- Stapler

Preparation:

Reproduce the poem *My Teddy Bear* and staple it to the right side of the white construction paper.

Procedure:

1. Children color the teddy bear brown leaving the bottom of paws and nose white.
2. Children cut out the teddy bear.
3. With teacher guidance, children glue on wiggly eyes, pompon nose, and 3 buttons.
4. Let dry.
5. Staple teddy bear to left side of the white construction paper.
6. Send the poem and art activity home. This gives family members an opportunity to reread the poem with the child, reinforcing the letter Tt.

CONCLUSION OF LESSON

Remind children they have learned to recognize letter Tt and they can think of words that have Tt in the initial position.

My Teddy Bear

I have a little teddy bear,

whose fur is soft and brown.

When I go to sleep at night,

he helps me settle down.

I take him everyplace I go,

My special friend,

I love him so!

My Teddy Bear

I have a little teddy bear,

whose fur is soft and brown.

When I go to sleep at night,

he helps me settle down.

I take him everyplace I go,

My special friend,

I love him so!

©1995 by Roberta Seckler Brown and Susan Carey

BLACKLINE MASTER—POEM

BLACKLINE MASTER—TEDDY BEAR

LESSON 2

Objective:

Children will read *My Tt Book* using 1-1 match.

Materials:

- Big Book—*My Tt Book* (see directions p. xi)
- Large poem—*My Teddy Bear* (see directions p. x)
- Little books—*My Tt Book* (see directions p. xi)
- Crayons

Procedure:

1. Introduce the lesson with the poem *My Teddy Bear*.
2. You reread the poem *My Teddy Bear* modeling 1-1 match with a pointer. Children echo read the poem and act it out.
3. You hold up the "big book," *My Tt Book.* You read the title. Children echo read.
4. You go through each page of the "big book," covering all print. You name the picture on the page. Tell the children to listen for Tt words.
5. You read through the "big book" one time, modeling 1-1 match and directionality.
6. Invite the children to now read the "big book" with you. Model 1-1 match and directionality while reading.
7. The children read through the book a third time while you point to the words.

INDEPENDENT ACTIVITY

1. Reproduce blackline master of the little *My Tt Book*. Give children their own little *My Tt Book* and have them color it in.
2. After children color in their own little *My Tt Book,* they read their book to a partner. ·
3. You monitor the activity, looking for 1-1 match and directionality.
4. Collect the books.

CONCLUSION OF LESSON

1. You gather the whole group back together for whole group instruction.
2. Everyone rereads the "big book," *My Tt Book,* together.
3. While the children are reading the "big book," you model 1-1 match and directionality, while pointing to the words.

My Tt Book

_____

(name)

- -

Can you find the turtle?

Can you find the tiger?

- -

Can you find the turkey?

Can you find the teddy bear?

Here they are!

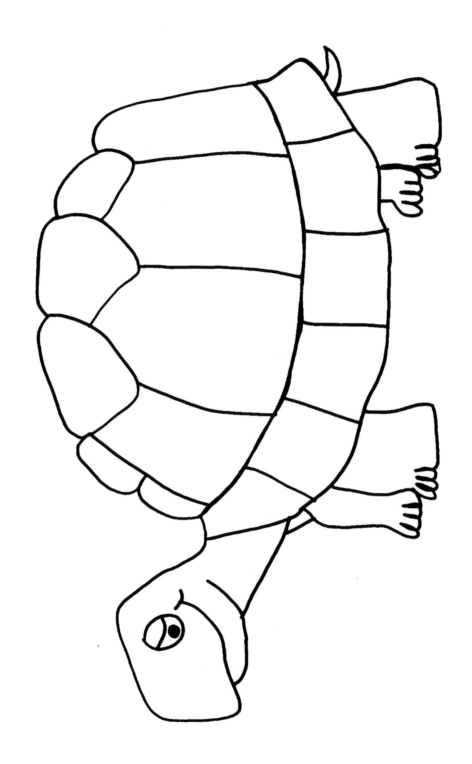

F

LESSON 3

Objective:

Child will focus on the 4 main cueing systems while reading little book, *My Tt Book.*

Materials:

▮ Big Book—*My Tt Book*
▮ Little books—*My Tt Book*
▮ Awards (see directions p. xii)
▮ Safety pins

Procedure:

1. Introduce the lesson with the Big book *My Tt Book.*
2. You read the "big book" with the children, modeling 1-1 match and directionality while pointing to the words.
3. Echo read the book.

INDIVIDUALIZED INSTRUCTION

Note—The objective is to focus the child on the 4 main cueing systems:

▮ Meaning
▮ Visual
▮ Structure
▮ 1-1 Match

(See page viii for definition and more information.)

1. You now take each child, one at a time, having him/her read the little book, *My Tt Book,* to you. Child points to words while reading.
2. As the child is reading to you, you are listening for misread text and prompting the child with the appropriate question to help him/her correct the error. Your phrasing of the questions must be consistent with those in the "Examples of Misread Text."
3. Through repeated use of these techniques, the children will begin to ask themselves these questions. This indicates the child is now monitoring his/her own reading and is on the way to becoming an independent reader.
4. Following are specific examples of misread text by a child using little *My Tt Book.* Find the type of example that matches what your student has read. After using the appropriate strategy questions and the child still

cannot recall the word, then tell the child the word! Teach the child right from the start that reading is *not* a trick!

5. The child's response may not be an exact match to the example. However, if the response is a similar mistake, prompt the child with the appropriate question.

Examples of Misread Text

Following are specific examples of misread text by a child using little *My Tt Book.* Find the type of example that matches what your student has read. Keep in mind that the child's response may not be an exact match to the example. However, if the response is a similar mistake, prompt the child with the appropriate question.

WHEN TO USE MEANING QUESTIONS

Objective:

Child must determine if what he/she has read makes sense in relation to the picture and in the context of the book they he/she is reading.

Example

Child reads:	Can you find the bear?
Text reads:	Can you find the teddy bear?

Strategy

Teacher:	"Does bear make sense in a Tt book?"
Child:	"No."
Teacher:	"What else could you try?"
Child:	"Teddy bear."
Teacher:	"Good! Teddy bear begins with t. *Good readers reread.*"

WHEN TO USE STRUCTURE QUESTIONS

Objective:

Child must be able to hear what he/she has read and determine if it sounds right grammatically.

Example

Child reads: Can you find these tiger?
Text reads: Can you find the tiger?

Strategy

Teacher: "Does that sound right? Is that how people talk?"
Child: "No."
Teacher: "What would sound right?"
Child: "Can you find the tiger?"
Teacher: "Good! *Good readers reread.*"

WHEN TO USE VISUAL QUESTIONS

Objective:
Child will use letter in the initial position to read a word in context.

Example

Child reads: Can you find the chicken?
Text reads: Can you find the turkey?

Strategy

You point to the misread word: "What sound does the letter t make?"
Child: "Tttt."
Teacher: "Reread."
Child: "Can you find the turkey?"
If the child hesitates and cannot recall the word, give it! Then have the child reread.

WHEN TO USE 1-1 QUESTIONS

Objective:

Child must understand what he/she says has to match the number of words on the page.

Example 1

Child reads: Can you find the scary tiger?
Text reads: Can you find the tiger?

Strategy

Teacher: "Did your finger match the words?"

Child: "No."

Teacher: "Reread."

If the finger does not match the second time, you take the child's finger and point to the words together.

Example 2

Child reads: Can you find turtle?
Text reads: Can you find the turtle?

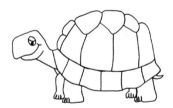

Strategy

Teacher: "Did your finger match the words?"

Child: "No."

Teacher: "Reread."

If the child responds, "Yes, my finger did match," take the child's finger and point to the words together.

LETTER Tt AWARD

When the child has successfully read his/her own *My Tt Book* to you, reward the child with an award. Copy and cut out the one shown here. Pin the award to the child's clothes.

I can read
<u>My Tt Book</u>.
Just ask me!

_____
(name)

CONCLUSION OF LESSON

Remind the child to leave the award on until a grown-up at home asks him/her to read the book.

LETTER

Uu

LESSON 1

Objective:

Child will

▪ visually recognize letter by name.

▪ recognize the sound /u/ in the initial position by naming words with u in that position.

Materials:

▪ Large chart with poem, *Little Umbrella* (see directions on p. x)

▪ Any alphabet card with the letter Uu

▪ Letter Uu can, containing such items as:
  – magazine picture of umpire
  – toy umbrella and unicorn
  – baby's undershirt

Procedure:

STEP 1

1. Introduce the lesson with the poem, *Little Umbrella.*

2. Display the poem on an easel. You read the poem modeling 1-1 match with a pointer.

387

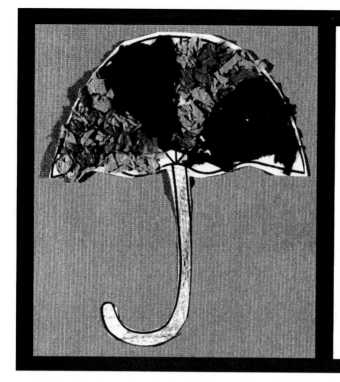

Little Umbrella

I have a little umbrella.
It helps me stay dry.
And on a very windy day,
it even helps me fly.
Open it. Close it.
Open it. Close it.
What fun it can be!
Jumping over puddles,
My little umbrella and me!

3. Ask the whole group, "What letter of the alphabet do you think we are studying now?"
4. Ask children to echo read the poem several times.
5. Ask children for suggestions of movements for acting out the poem.
6. Reread the poem together, acting it out!
7. Put the poem aside.

STEP 2

1. Display the alphabet card with the letter Uu.
2. Ask children to name the letter they see on the alphabet card.
3. Hold up the letter Uu can.
4. Ask children to predict what would make sense in a Uu can.
5. Take each object/picture out of the can. Name them.
6. Ask children to repeat the name of each object/picture after you name it.
7. Show children a sample of the art activity.

8. You now do the art activity with the children, either as a small group or whole class.

ART ACTIVITY

Little Umbrella

Materials:

- Blackline master of poem *Little Umbrella*
- Blackline master of umbrella
- Crayons
- Blue construction paper 12″ × 18″
- 2″ squares of tissue paper (assorted colors)
- Scissors
- Glue
- Stapler

Preparation:

Reproduce the poem *Little Umbrella* and staple it to the right side of the blue construction paper.

Procedure:

1. Children color the handle of the umbrella.
2. Children cut out the umbrella.
3. With teacher guidance, children roll tissue paper into small balls and glue onto blackline of umbrella.
4. Let dry.
5. Staple umbrella to left side of the blue construction paper.
6. Send the poem and art activity home. This gives family members an opportunity to reread the poem with the child, reinforcing the letter Uu.

CONCLUSION OF LESSON

Remind children they have learned to recognize letter Uu and they can think of words that have Uu in the initial position.

Little Umbrella

I have a little umbrella.

It helps me to stay dry.

And on a very windy day,

it even helps me fly.

Open it. Close it. Open it.

Close it. What fun it can be!

Jumping over puddles.

My little umbrella–and me!

- -

Little Umbrella

I have a little umbrella.

It helps me to stay dry.

And on a very windy day,

it even helps me fly.

Open it. Close it. Open it.

Close it. What fun it can be!

Jumping over puddles.

My little umbrella–and me!

BLACKLINE MASTER—POEM

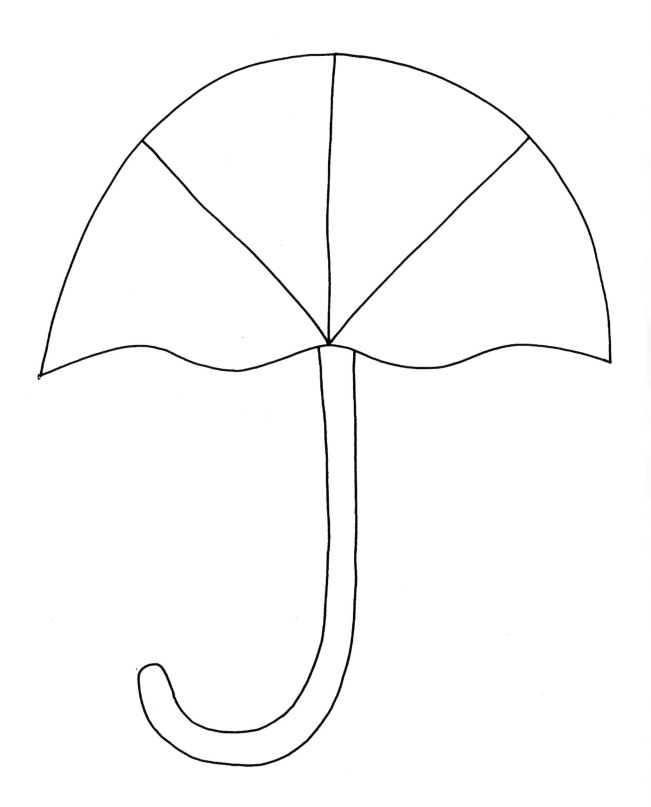

BLACKLINE MASTER—UMBRELLA

391

LESSON 2

Objective:

Children will read *My Uu Book* using 1-1 match.

Materials:

- Big Book—*My Uu Book* (see directions p. xi)
- Large poem—*Little Umbrella* (see directions p. x)
- Little books—*My Uu Book* (see directions p. xi)
- Crayons

Procedure:

1. Introduce the lesson with the poem *Little Umbrella.*
2. You reread the poem *Little Umbrella* modeling 1-1 match with a pointer. Children echo read the poem and act it out.
3. You hold up the "big book," *My Uu Book.* You read the title. Children echo read.
4. You go through each page of the "big book," covering all print. You name the picture on the page. Tell the children to listen for Uu words.
5. You read through the "big book" one time, modeling 1-1 match and directionality.
6. Invite the children to now read the "big book" with you. Model 1-1 match and directionality while reading.
7. The children read through the book a third time while you point to the words.

INDEPENDENT ACTIVITY

1. Reproduce blackline master of the little *My Uu Book.* Give children their own little *My Uu Book* and have them color it in.
2. After children color in their own little *My Uu Book,* they read their book to a partner.
3. You monitor the activity, looking for 1-1 match and directionality.
4. Collect the books.

CONCLUSION OF LESSON

1. You gather the whole group back together for whole group instruction.
2. Everyone rereads the "big book," *My Uu Book,* together.
3. While the children are reading the "big book," you model 1-1 match and directionality, while pointing to the words.

My Uu Book

_____
(name)

- -

See the umpire.

See the umbrella.

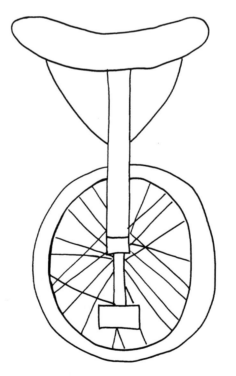

See the unicycle.

See the unicorn.

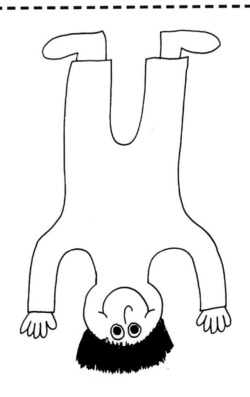

See me. Upside down!

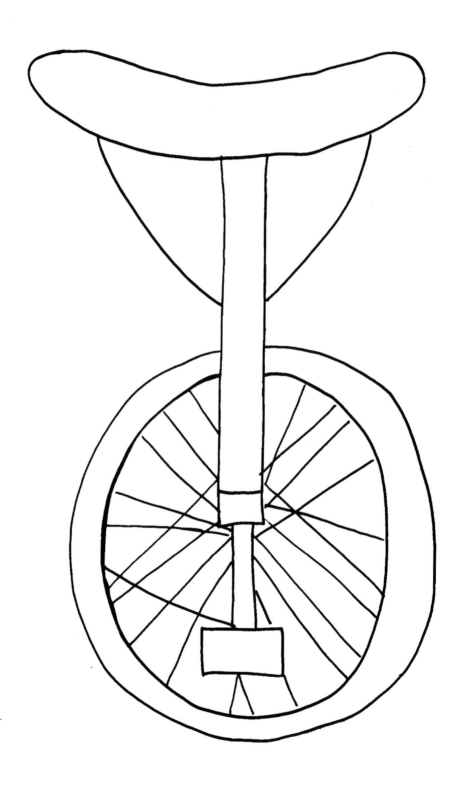

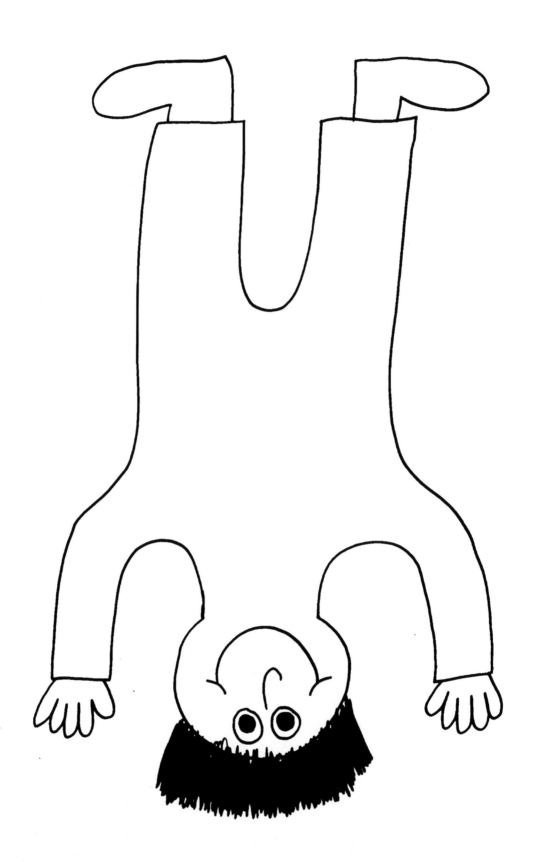

LESSON 3

Objective:

Child will focus on the 4 main cueing systems while reading little book, *My Uu Book.*

Materials:

▪ Big Book—*My Uu Book*
▪ Little books—*My Uu Book*
▪ Awards (see directions p. xii)
▪ Safety pins

Procedure:

1. Introduce the lesson with the "big book," *My Uu Book.*
2. You read the "big book" with the children, modeling 1-1 match and directionality while pointing to the words.
3. Echo read the book.

INDIVIDUALIZED INSTRUCTION

Note—The objective is to focus the child on the 4 main cueing systems:

▪ Meaning
▪ Visual
▪ Structure
▪ 1-1 Match

(See page viii for definition and more information.)

1. You now take each child, one at a time, having him/her read the little book, *My Uu Book,* to you. Child points to words while reading.
2. As the child is reading to you, you are listening for misread text and prompting the child with the appropriate question to help him/her correct the error. Your phrasing of the questions must be consistent with those in the "Examples of Misread Text."
3. Through repeated use of these techniques, the children will begin to ask themselves these questions. This indicates the child is now monitoring his/her own reading and is on the way to becoming an independent reader.
4. Following are specific examples of misread text by a child using little *My Uu Book.* Find the type of example that matches what your student has read. After using the appropriate strategy questions and the child still

cannot recall the word, then tell the child the word! Teach the child right from the start that reading is *not* a trick!

5. The child's response may not be an exact match to the example. However, if the response is a similar mistake, prompt the child with the appropriate question.

Examples of Misread Text

Following are specific examples of misread text by a child using little *My Uu Book*. Find the type of example that matches what your student has read. Keep in mind that the child's response may not be an exact match to the example. However, if the response is a similar mistake, prompt the child with the appropriate question.

WHEN TO USE MEANING QUESTIONS

Objective:

Child must determine if what he/she has read makes sense in relation to the picture and in the context of the book he/she is reading.

Example

Child reads: See the horse.
Text reads: See the unicorn.

Strategy

Teacher: "Look at the picture. Is that a horse?"

Child: "No. It's a unicorn."

Teacher: "Good! *Good readers reread.*"

WHEN TO USE STRUCTURE QUESTIONS

Objective:

Child must be able to hear what he/she has read and determine if it sounds right grammatically.

Example

Child reads:	Seen the unicycle.
Text reads:	See the unicycle.

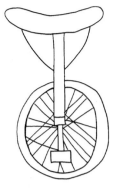

Strategy

Teacher:	"Does that sound right? Is that how people talk?"
Child:	"No."
Teacher:	"What would sound right?"
Child:	"See the unicycle."
Teacher:	"Good! *Good readers reread.*"

WHEN TO USE VISUAL QUESTIONS

Objective:

Child will use letter in the initial position to read a word in context.

Example

Child reads:	See the man.
Text reads:	See the umpire.

Strategy

You point to the misread word: "What word do you know that starts with the letter u and makes sense?"

Child:	"Umpire."
Teacher:	"Reread."

If the child hesitates and cannot recall the word, give it! Then have the child reread.

WHEN TO USE 1-1 QUESTIONS

Objective:

Child must understand what he/she says has to match the number of words on the page.

Example 1

Child reads: See me up side down.
Text reads: See me. Upside down!

Strategy

Teacher: "Did your finger match the words?"

Child: "No."

Teacher: "Reread."

If the finger does not match the second time, you take the child's finger and point to the words together.

Example 2

Child reads: The umbrella.
Text reads: See the umbrella.

Strategy

Teacher: "Did your finger match the words?"

Child: "No."

Teacher: "Reread."

If the child responds, "Yes, my finger did match," take the child's finger and point to the words together.

LETTER Uu AWARD

When the child has successfully read his/her own *My Uu Book* to you, reward the child with an award. Copy and cut out the one shown here. Pin the award to the child's clothes.

I can read
<u>My Uu Book</u>.
Just ask me!

_____
(name)

<u>CONCLUSION OF LESSON</u>

Remind the child to leave the award on until a grown-up at home asks him/her to read the book.

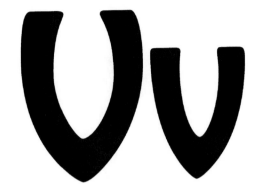

LETTER

LESSON 1

Objective:

Child will

▮ visually recognize letter by name.

▮ recognize the sound /v/ in the initial position by naming words with v in that position.

Materials:

▮ Large chart with poem, *Vegetables* (see directions on p. x)

▮ Any alphabet card with the letter Vv

▮ Letter Vv can, containing such items as:
  – magazine pictures of vacuums, vines, and volcanoes
  – plastic vegetables
  – small piece of velcro

Procedure:

STEP 1

1. Introduce the lesson with the poem, *Vegetables.*

2. Display the poem on an easel. You read the poem modeling 1-1 match with a pointer.

Vegetables

Vegetables are good for you,
They make you strong and
healthy, too.
If you eat them everyday,
"I feel so good!" is what you'll say.
Carrots, corn, string beans, too.
All of these are good for you!

3. Ask the whole group, "What letter of the alphabet do you think we are studying now?"
4. Ask children to echo read the poem several times.
5. Ask children for suggestions of movements for acting out the poem.
6. Reread the poem together, acting it out!
7. Put the poem aside.

STEP 2

1. Display the alphabet card with the letter Vv.
2. Ask children to name the letter they see on the alphabet card.
3. Hold up the letter Vv can.
4. Ask children to predict what would make sense in a Vv can.
5. Take each object/picture out of the can. Name them.
6. Ask children to repeat the name of each object/picture after you name it.

7. Show children a sample of the art activity.
8. You now do the art activity with the children, either as a small group or whole class.

ART ACTIVITY

Vegetable Platter

Materials:

■ Blackline master of poem *Vegetables*
■ Blackline master of vegetables
■ Crayons
■ Scissors
■ Yellow construction paper 12″ × 18″
■ 12″ round white paper plate
■ Stapler

Preparation:

Reproduce the poem *Vegetables* and staple it to the right side of the yellow construction paper.

Procedure:

1. Children color blackline of vegetables.
2. Then they cut the vegetables out and glue on to the paper plate.
3. You staple "vegetable platter" to yellow construction paper with poem.
4. Send the poem and art activity home. This gives family members an opportunity to reread the poem with the child, reinforcing the letter Vv.

CONCLUSION OF LESSON

Remind children they have learned to recognize letter Vv and they can think of words that have Vv in the initial position.

Vegetables

Vegetables are good for you!

They make you strong,

and healthy too.

If you eat them everyday,

"I feel so good!"

is what you'll say. Carrots,

corn, string beans, too.

All of these are good for you!

- -

Vegetables

Vegetables are good for you!

They make you strong,

and healthy too.

If you eat them everyday,

"I feel so good!"

is what you'll say. Carrots,

corn, string beans, too.

All of these are good for you!

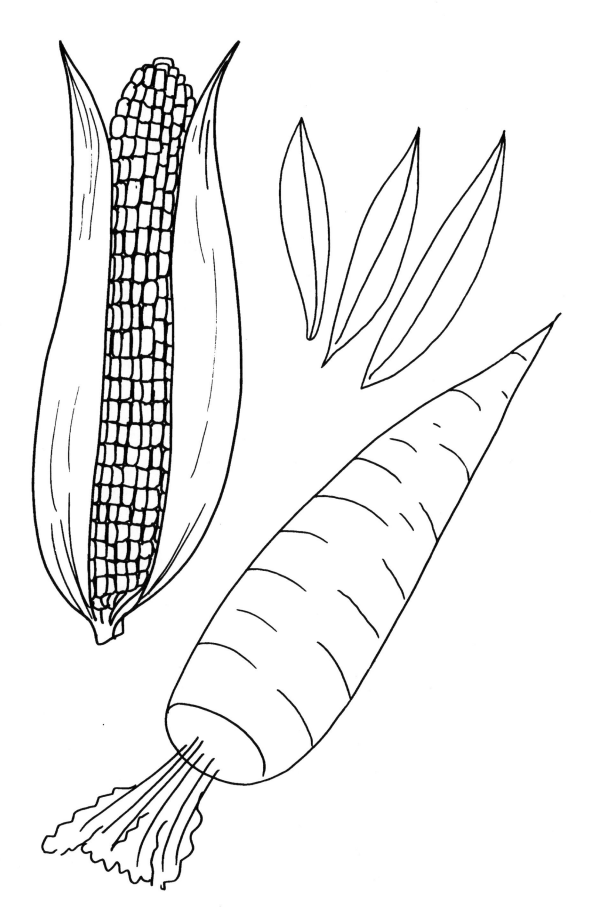

LESSON 2

Objective:

Children will read *My Vv Book* using 1-1 match.

Materials:

- Big Book—*My Vv Book* (see directions p. xi)
- Large poem—*Vegetables* (see directions p. x)
- Little books—*My Vv Book* (see directions p. xi)
- Crayons

Procedure:

1. Introduce the lesson with the poem *Vegetables.*
2. You reread the poem *Vegetables* modeling 1-1 match with a pointer. Children echo read the poem and act it out.
3. You hold up the "big book," *My Vv Book.* You read the title. Children echo read.
4. You go through each page of the "big book," covering all print. You name the picture on the page. Tell the children to listen for Vv words.
5. You read through the "big book" one time, modeling 1-1 match and directionality.
6. Invite the children to now read the "big book" with you. Model 1-1 match and directionality while reading.
7. The children read through the book a third time while you point to the words.

INDEPENDENT ACTIVITY

1. Reproduce blackline master of the little *My Vv Book.* Give children their own little *My Vv Book* and have them color it in.
2. After children color in their own little *My Vv Book,* they read their book to a partner.
3. You monitor the activity, looking for 1-1 match and directionality.
4. Collect the books.

CONCLUSION OF LESSON

1. You gather the whole group back together for whole group instruction.
2. Everyone rereads the "big book," *My Vv Book,* together.
3. While the children are reading the "big book," you model 1-1 match and directionality, while pointing to the words.

My Vv Book

_____

(name)

- -

Look at the volcano.

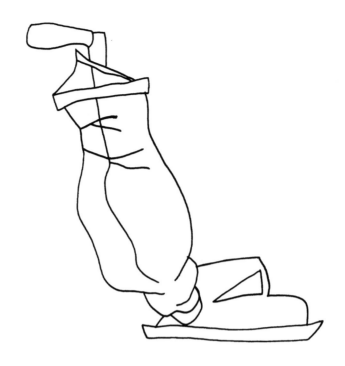

Look at the vacuum.

Look at the violin.

Look at the vine.

- -

Love

Look at the valentine.
For you!

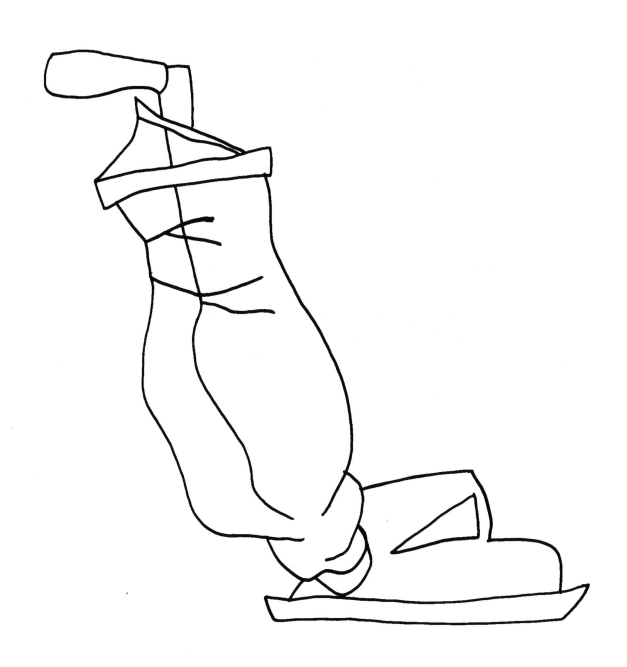

F

LESSON 3

Objective:

Child will focus on the 4 main cueing systems while reading little book, *My Vv Book.*

Materials:

- Big Book—*My Vv Book*
- Little books—*My Vv Book*
- Awards (see directions p. xii)
- Safety pins

Procedure:

1. Introduce the lesson with the "big book," *My Vv Book.*
2. You read the "big book" with the children, modeling 1-1 match and directionality while pointing to the words.
3. Echo read the book.

INDIVIDUALIZED INSTRUCTION

Note—The objective is to focus the child on the 4 main cueing systems:

- Meaning
- Visual
- Structure
- 1-1 Match

(See page viii for definition and more information.)

1. You now take each child, one at a time, having him/her read the little book, *My Vv Book,* to you. Child points to words while reading.
2. As the child is reading to you, you are listening for misread text and prompting the child with the appropriate question to help him/her correct the error. Your phrasing of the questions must be consistent with those in the "Examples of Misread Text."
3. Through repeated use of these techniques, the children will begin to ask themselves these questions. This indicates the child is now monitoring his/her own reading and is on the way to becoming an independent reader.
4. Following are specific examples of misread text by a child using little *My Vv Book.* Find the type of example that matches what your student has read. After using the appropriate strategy questions and the child still

cannot recall the word, then tell the child the word! Teach the child right from the start that reading is *not* a trick!

5. The child's response may not be an exact match to the example. However, if the response is a similar mistake, prompt the child with the appropriate question.

Examples of Misread Text

Following are specific examples of misread text by a child using little *My Vv Book*. Find the type of example that matches what your student has read. Keep in mind that the child's response may not be an exact match to the example. However, if the response is a similar mistake, prompt the child with the appropriate question.

WHEN TO USE MEANING QUESTIONS

Objective:

Child must determine if what he/she has read makes sense in relation to the picture and in the context of the book he/she is reading.

Example

Child reads:	Look at the weed.
Text reads:	Look at the vine.

Strategy

Teacher:	"Does the weed make sense in a Vv book?"
Child:	"No."
Teacher:	"What else could you try?"
Child:	"Vine."
Teacher:	"Good! Vine begins with v. *Good readers reread.*"

WHEN TO USE STRUCTURE QUESTIONS

Objective:

Child must be able to hear what he/she has read and determine if it sounds right grammatically.

Example

Child reads: Like at the vacuum.
Text reads: Look at the vacuum.

Strategy

Teacher: "Does that sound right? Is that how people talk?"

Child: "No."

Teacher: "What would sound right?"

Child: "Look at the vacuum."

Teacher: "Good! *Good readers reread.*"

WHEN TO USE VISUAL QUESTIONS

Objective:

Child will use letter in the initial position to read a word in context.

Example

Child reads: Look at the mountain.
Text reads: Look at the volcano.

Strategy

You point to the misread word: "What sound does the letter v make?"

Child: "Vvvv."

Teacher: "Reread."

If the child hesitates and cannot recall the word, give it! Then have the child reread.

WHEN TO USE 1-1 QUESTIONS

Objective:

Child must understand what he/she says has to match the number of words on the page.

Example 1

Child reads: Look at the valentine. It's for you!
Text reads: Look at the valentine. For you!

Strategy

Teacher: "Did your finger match the words?"

Child: "No."

Teacher: "Reread."

If the finger does not match the second time, you take the child's finger and point to the words together.

Example 2

Child reads: Look at violin.
Text reads: Look at the violin.

Strategy

Teacher: "Did your finger match the words?"

Child: "No."

Teacher: "Reread."

If the child responds, "Yes, my finger did match," take the child's finger and point to the words together.

LETTER Vv AWARD

When the child has successfully read his/her own *My Vv Book* to you, reward the child with an award. Copy and cut out the one shown here. Pin the award to the child's clothes.

I can read
<u>My Vv Book</u>.
Just ask me!

_____
(name)

<u>CONCLUSION OF LESSON</u>

Remind the child to leave the award on until a grown-up at home asks him/her to read the book.

LETTER

LESSON 1

Objective:

Child will

- visually recognize letter by name.
- recognize the sound /w/ in the initial position by naming words with w in that position.

Materials:

- Large chart with poem, *Wild Whales* (see directions on p. x)
- Any alphabet card with the letter Ww
- Letter Ww can, containing such items as:
  - rubber worm
  - watch
  - whistle
  - toy whale
  - walnut

Procedure:

STEP 1

1. Introduce the lesson with the poem, *Wild Whales.*
2. Display the poem on an easel. You read the poem modeling 1-1 match with a pointer.

427

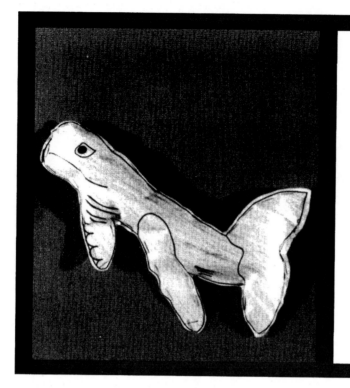

Wild Whales

A whale is a mammal,
that lives in the sea.
No other animal is quite as
big as he.
When he comes up for air,
water *shoots* out his spout.
So graceful, this giant
jumping in and out.

3. Ask the whole group, "What letter of the alphabet do you think we are studying now?"
4. Ask children to echo read the poem several times.
5. Ask children for suggestions of movements for acting out the poem.
6. Reread the poem together, acting it out!
7. Put the poem aside.

STEP 2

1. Display the alphabet card with the letter Ww.
2. Ask children to name the letter they see on the alphabet card.
3. Hold up the letter Ww can.
4. Ask children to predict what would make sense in a Ww can.
5. Take each object/picture out of the can. Name them.
6. Ask children to repeat the name of each object/picture after you name it.
7. Show children a sample of the art activity.

8. You now do the art activity with the children, either as a small group or whole class.

ART ACTIVITY

Stuffed Whales

Materials:

■ Blackline master of poem *Wild Whales*
■ Blackline master of whale
■ Blue and gray crayons
■ Blue construction paper 12" × 18"
■ White construction paper 8-1/2" × 11"
■ 4 bags of poly-fill per class of 20
■ Stapler

Preparation:

Reproduce the poem *Wild Whales* and staple it to the right side of the blue construction paper. You staple the blackline of the whale and sheet of white paper together (one set per child). Staples are placed all around the whale outline, leaving room for stuffing.

Procedure:

1. Children color the whale using blue or gray crayons.
2. Children cut out the whale on the outside of the staples.
3. With teacher guidance, children stuff the whale.
4. You staple the rest of the whale.
5. Staple whale to left side of the blue construction paper.
6. Send the poem and art activity home. This gives family members an opportunity to reread the poem with the child, reinforcing the letter Ww.

CONCLUSION OF LESSON

Remind children they have learned to recognize letter Ww and they can think of words that have Ww in the initial position.

Wild Whales

A whale is a mammal,

that lives in the sea.

No other animal is

quite as big as he.

When he comes up for air,

water *shoots* out his spout.

So graceful, this giant

jumping in and out.

- -

Wild Whales

A whale is a mammal,

that lives in the sea.

No other animal is

quite as big as he.

When he comes up for air,

water *shoots* out his spout.

So graceful, this giant

jumping in and out.

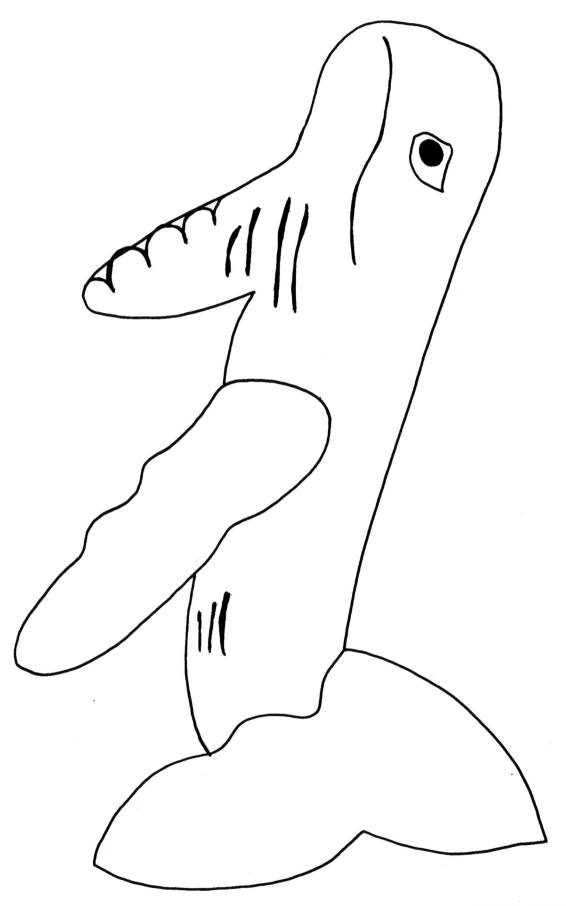

BLACKLINE MASTER—WHALE

LESSON 2

Objective:

Children will read *My Ww Book* using 1-1 match.

Materials:

■ Big Book—*My Ww Book* (see directions p. xi)
■ Large poem—*Wild Whales* (see directions p. x)
■ Little books—*My Ww Book* (see directions p. xi)
■ Crayons

Procedure:

1. Introduce the lesson with the poem *Wild Whales.*
2. You reread the poem *Wild Whales* modeling 1-1 match with a pointer. Children echo read the poem and act it out.
3. You hold up the "big book," *My Ww Book.* You read the title. Children echo read.
4. You go through each page of the "big book," covering all print. You name the picture on the page. Tell the children to listen for Ww words.
5. You read through the "big book" one time, modeling 1-1 match and directionality.
6. Invite the children to now read the "big book" with you. Model 1-1 match and directionality while reading.
7. The children read through the book a third time while you point to the words.

INDEPENDENT ACTIVITY

1. Reproduce blackline master of the little *My Ww Book.* Give children their own little *My Ww Book* and have them color it in.
2. After children color in their own little *My Ww Book,* they read their book to a partner.
3. You monitor the activity, looking for 1-1 match and directionality.
4. Collect the books.

CONCLUSION OF LESSON

1. You gather the whole group back together for whole group instruction.
2. Everyone rereads the "big book," *My Ww Book,* together.
3. While the children are reading the "big book," you model 1-1 match and directionality, while pointing to the words.

My Ww Book

_____

(name)

The watch can tick.

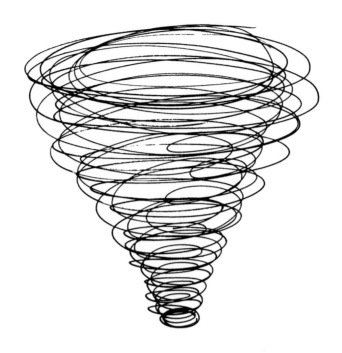

The wind can whirl.

- -

The window can open.

The whale can swim.

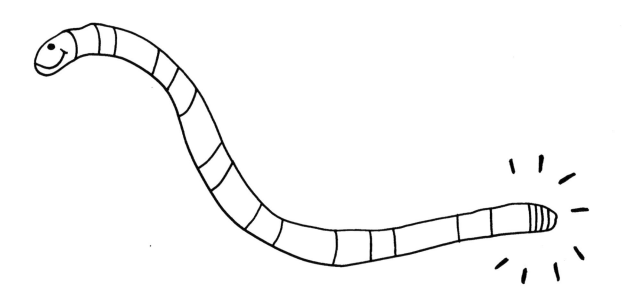

The worm can wiggle.
Wiggle-waggle!

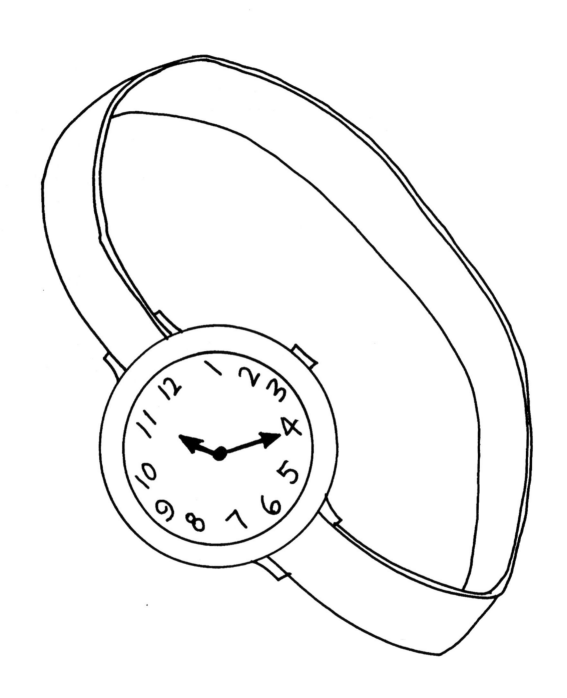

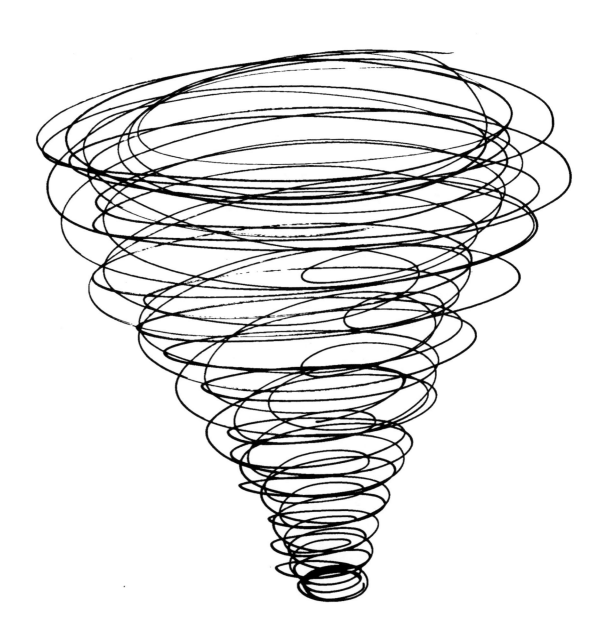

F

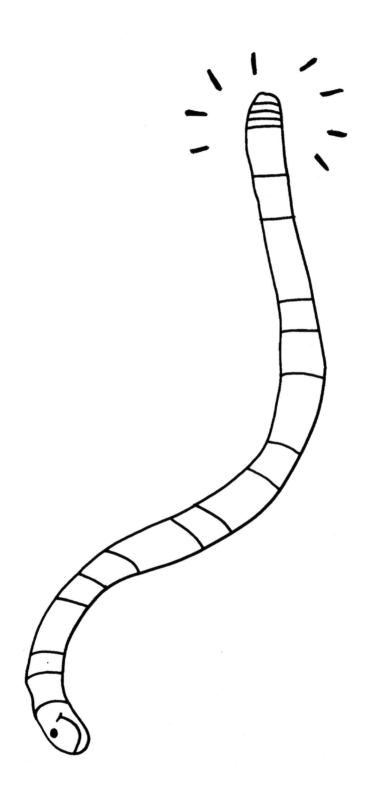

LESSON 3

Objective:

Child will focus on the 4 main cueing systems while reading little book, *My Ww Book.*

Materials:

▮ Big Book—*My Ww Book*
▮ Little books—*My Ww Book*
▮ Awards (see directions p. xii)
▮ Safety pins

Procedure:

1. Introduce the lesson with the "big book," *My Ww Book.*
2. You read the "big book" with the children, modeling 1-1 match and directionality while pointing to the words.
3. Echo read the book.

INDIVIDUALIZED INSTRUCTION

Note—The objective is to focus the child on the 4 main cueing systems:

▮ Meaning
▮ Visual
▮ Structure
▮ 1-1 Match

(See page viii for definition and more information.)

1. You now take each child, one at a time, having him/her read the little book, *My Ww Book,* to you. Child points to words while reading.
2. As the child is reading to you, you are listening for misread text and prompting the child with the appropriate question to help him/her correct the error. Your phrasing of the questions must be consistent with those in the "Examples of Misread Text."
3. Through repeated use of these techniques, the children will begin to ask themselves these questions. This indicates the child is now monitoring his/her own reading and is on the way to becoming an independent reader.
4. Following are specific examples of misread text by a child using little *My Ww Book.* Find the type of example that matches what your student has read. After using the appropriate strategy questions and the child still

cannot recall the word, then tell the child the word! Teach the child right from the start that reading is *not* a trick!

5. The child's response may not be an exact match to the example. However, if the response is a similar mistake, prompt the child with the appropriate question.

Examples of Misread Text

Following are specific examples of misread text by a child using little *My Ww Book.* Find the type of example that matches what your student has read. Keep in mind that the child's response may not be an exact match to the example. However, if the response is a similar mistake, prompt the child with the appropriate question.

WHEN TO USE MEANING QUESTIONS

Objective:

Child must determine if what he/she has read makes sense in relation to the picture and in the context of the book he/she is reading.

Example

Child reads:	The clock can tick.
Text reads:	The watch can tick.

Strategy

Teacher:	"Look at the picture. Is that a clock?"
Child:	"No. It's a watch."
Teacher:	"Good! *Good readers reread.*"

WHEN TO USE STRUCTURE QUESTIONS

Objective:

Child must be able to hear what he/she has read and determine if it sounds right grammatically.

Example

Child reads: The whale could swim.
Text reads: The whale can swim.

Strategy

Teacher: "Does that sound right? Is that how people talk?"

Child: "No."

Teacher: "What would sound right?"

Child: "The whale can swim."

Teacher: "Good! *Good readers reread.*"

WHEN TO USE VISUAL QUESTIONS

Objective:

Child will use letter in the initial position to read a word in context.

Example

Child reads: The tornado can whirl.
Text reads: The wind can whirl.

Strategy

You point to the misread word: "What sound does the letter w make?"

Child: "Wwww."

Teacher: "Reread."

Child: "The wind can whirl."

If the child hesitates and cannot recall the word, give it! Then have the child reread.

WHEN TO USE 1-1 QUESTIONS

Objective:

Child must understand what he/she says has to match the number of words on the page.

Example 1

Child reads: The window opens.
Text reads: The window can open.

Strategy

Teacher: "Did your finger match the words?"

Child: "No."

Teacher: "Reread."

If the finger does not match the second time, you take the child's finger and point to the words together.

Example 2

Child reads: The watch can tick tock.
Text reads: The watch can tick.

Strategy

Teacher: "Did your finger match the words?"

Child: "No."

Teacher: "Reread."

If the child responds, "Yes, my finger did match," take the child's finger and point to the words together.

LETTER Ww AWARD

When the child has successfully read his/her own *My Ww Book* to you, reward the child with an award. Copy and cut out the one shown here. Pin the award to the child's clothes.

I can read
<u>My Ww Book</u>.
Just ask me!

_____
(name)

<u>CONCLUSION OF LESSON</u>

Remind the child to leave the award on until a grown-up at home asks him/her to read the book.

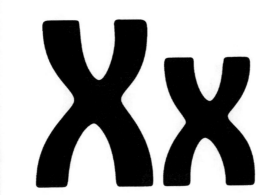

LETTER

Xx

LESSON 1

Objective:

Child will

- visually recognize letter by name.
- recognize the sound /x/ in the initial position by naming words with x in that position.

Materials:

- Large chart with poem, *X-rays* (see directions on p. x)
- Any alphabet card with the letter Xx
- Letter Xx can, containing such items as:
  - real x-rays

Procedure:

STEP 1

1. Introduce the lesson with the poem, *X-rays*.
2. Display the poem on an easel. You read the poem modeling 1-1 match with a pointer.
3. Ask the whole group, "What letter of the alphabet do you think we are studying now?"

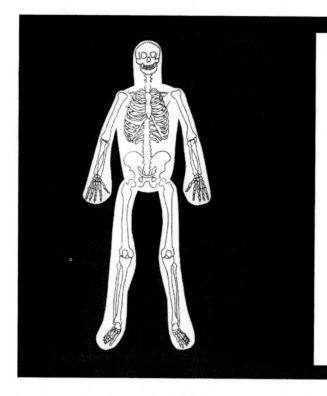

X-Rays

X-rays are pictures of bones inside.
You can count them,
none can hide.
X-rays let the doctor see,
If your bones are strong
and healthy.
Milk helps your bones
stay big and strong.
Drink a lot ...
You can't go wrong!

4. Ask children to echo read the poem several times.
5. Ask children for suggestions of movements for acting out the poem.
6. Reread the poem together, acting it out!
7. Put the poem aside.

STEP 2

1. Display the alphabet card with the letter Xx.
2. Ask children to name the letter they see on the alphabet card.
3. Hold up the letter Xx can.
4. Ask children to predict what would make sense in an Xx can.
5. Take each object/picture out of the can. Name them.
6. Ask children to repeat the name of each object/picture after you name it.

7. Show children a sample of the art activity.
8. You now do the art activity with the children, either as a small group or whole class.

ART ACTIVITY

X-ray Person

Materials:
- Blackline master of poem *X-rays*
- Blackline master of x-ray person
- Black construction paper 12″ × 18″
- Scissors
- Glue
- Stapler

Preparation:
Reproduce the poem *X-rays* and staple the poem to the right side of the black construction paper.

Procedure:
1. Children cut out each piece of the blackline of the x-ray person.
2. With teacher guidance, children glue x-ray person together on black paper.
3. Let dry.
4. Send the poem and art activity home. This gives family members an opportunity to reread the poem with the child, reinforcing the letter Xx.

CONCLUSION OF LESSON

Remind children they have learned to recognize letter Xx and they can think of words that have Xx in the initial position.

X-Rays

X-rays are pictures

of bones inside.

You can count them,

none can hide!

X-rays let the doctor see,

If your bones are strong

and healthy!

Milk helps your bones stay

big and strong. Drink a lot...

You can't go wrong!

X-Rays

X-rays are pictures

of bones inside.

You can count them,

none can hide!

X-rays let the doctor see,

If your bones are strong

and healthy!

Milk helps your bones stay

big and strong. Drink a lot...

You can't go wrong!

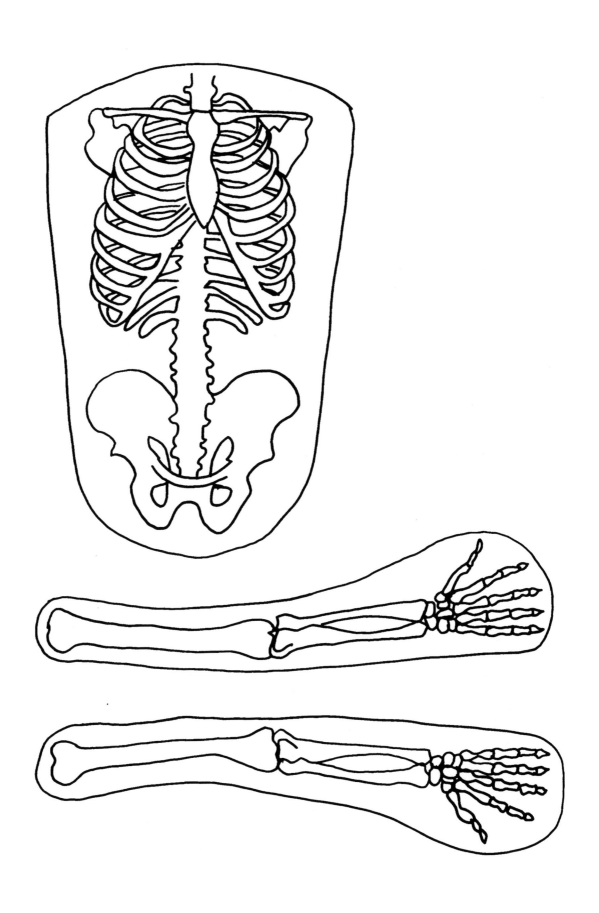

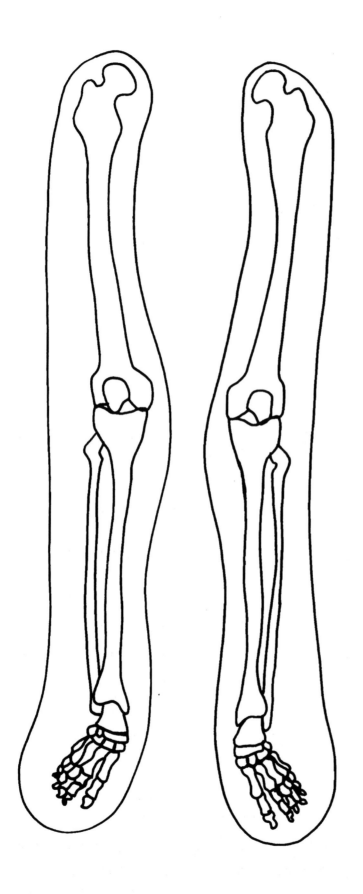

LESSON 2

Objective:

Children will read *My Xx Book* using 1-1 match.

Materials:

▪ Big Book—*My Xx Book* (see directions p. xi)
▪ Large poem—*X-rays* (see directions p. x)
▪ Little books—*My Xx Book* (see directions p. xi)
▪ Crayons

Procedure:

1. Introduce the lesson with the poem *X-rays.*
2. You reread the poem *X-rays* modeling 1-1 match with a pointer. Children echo read the poem and act it out.
3. You hold up the "big book," *My Xx Book.* You read the title. Children echo read.
4. You go through each page of the "big book," covering all print. You name the picture on the page. Tell the children to listen for Xx words.
5. You read through the "big book" one time, modeling 1-1 match and directionality.
6. Invite the children to now read the "big book" with you. Model 1-1 match and directionality while reading.
7. The children read through the book a third time while you point to the words.

INDEPENDENT ACTIVITY

1. Reproduce blackline master of the little *My Xx Book.* Give children their own little *My Xx Book* and have them color it in.
2. After children color in their own little *My Xx Book,* they read their book to a partner.
3. You monitor the activity, looking for 1-1 match and directionality.
4. Collect the books.

CONCLUSION OF LESSON

1. You gather the whole group back together for whole group instruction.
2. Everyone rereads the "big book," *My Xx Book,* together.
3. While the children are reading the "big book," you model 1-1 match and directionality, while pointing to the words.

S

My Xx Book

_____

(name)

- -

I see the head.

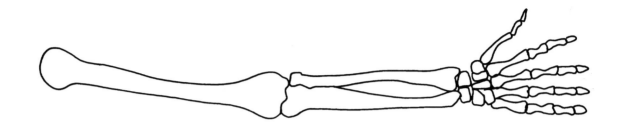

I see the arm.

- -

I see the leg.

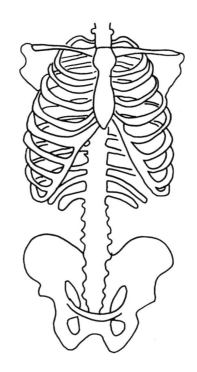

I see the torso.

- -

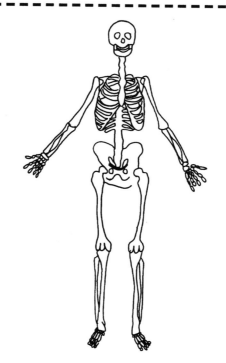

I see the x-ray... of my bones!

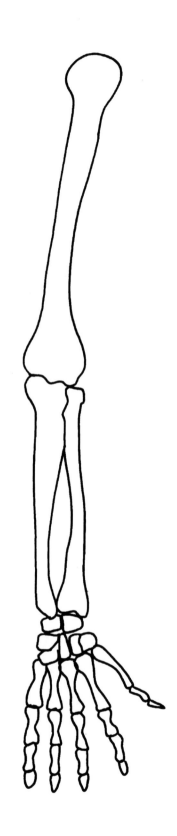

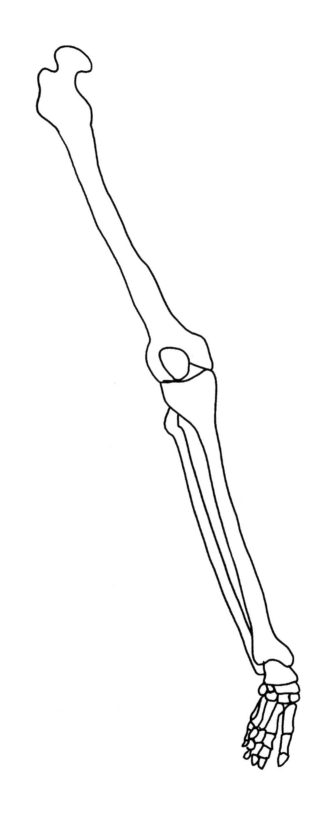

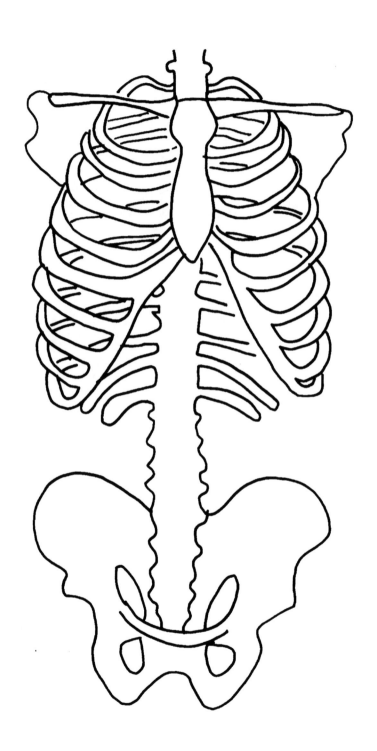

F

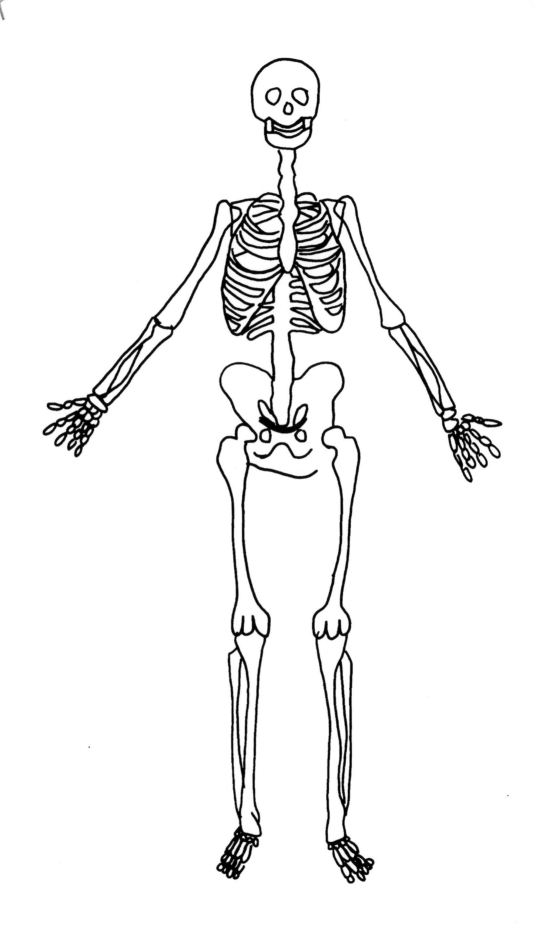

LESSON 3

Objective:

Child will focus on the 4 main cueing systems while reading little book, *My Xx Book.*

Materials:

- Big Book—*My Xx Book*
- Little books—*My Xx Book*
- Awards (see directions p. xii)
- Safety pins

Procedure:

1. Introduce the lesson with the "big book," *My Xx Book.*
2. You read the "big book" with the children, modeling 1-1 match and directionality while pointing to the words.
3. Echo read the book.

INDIVIDUALIZED INSTRUCTION

Note—The objective is to focus the child on the 4 main cueing systems:

- Meaning
- Visual
- Structure
- 1-1 Match

(See page viii for definition and more information.)

1. You now take each child, one at a time, having him/her read the little book, *My Xx Book,* to you. Child points to words while reading.
2. As the child is reading to you, you are listening for misread text and prompting the child with the appropriate question to help him/her correct the error. Your phrasing of the questions must be consistent with those in the "Examples of Misread Text."
3. Through repeated use of these techniques, the children will begin to ask themselves these questions. This indicates the child is now monitoring his/her own reading and is on the way to becoming an independent reader.
4. Following are specific examples of misread text by a child using little *My Xx Book.* Find the type of example that matches what your student has

read. After using the appropriate strategy questions and the child still cannot recall the word, then tell the child the word! Teach the child right from the start that reading is *not* a trick!

5. The child's response may not be an exact match to the example. However, if the response is a similar mistake, prompt the child with the appropriate question.

Examples of Misread Text

Following are specific examples of misread text by a child using little *My Xx Book.* Find the type of example that matches what your student has read. Keep in mind that the child's response may not be an exact match to the example. However, if the response is a similar mistake, prompt the child with the appropriate question.

WHEN TO USE MEANING QUESTIONS

Objective:

Child must determine if what he/she has read makes sense in relation to the picture and in the context of the book he/she is reading.

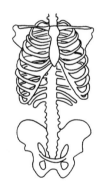

Example

Child reads:	I see the shape.
Text reads:	I see the torso.

Strategy

Teacher:	"Does shape make sense in book about x-rays?"
Child:	"No."
Teacher:	"Good! *Good readers reread.*"

WHEN TO USE STRUCTURE QUESTIONS

Objective:

Child must be able to hear what he/she has read and determine if it sounds right grammatically.

Example

Child reads: Me see the leg.
Text reads: I see the leg.

Strategy

Teacher: "Does that sound right? Is that how people talk?"
Child: "No."
Teacher: "What would sound right?"
Child: "I see the leg."
Teacher: "Good! *Good readers reread.*"

WHEN TO USE 1-1 QUESTIONS

Objective:

Child must understand what he/she says has to match the number of words on the page.

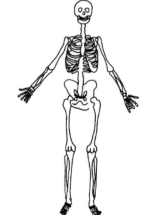

Example 1

Child reads: I see the x-ray of me.
Text reads: I see the x-ray of my bones!

Strategy

Teacher: "Did your finger match the words?"
Child: "No."
Teacher: "Reread."

If the finger does not match the second time, you take the child's finger and point to the words together.

Example 2

Child reads: I see the x-ray of all my bones.
Text reads: I see the x-ray ° of my bones!

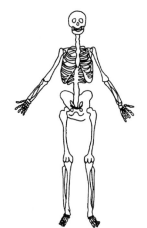

Strategy

Teacher: "Did your finger match the words?"

Child: "No."

Teacher: "Reread."

If the child responds, "Yes, my finger did match," take the child's finger and point to the words together.

LETTER Xx AWARD

When the child has successfully read his/her own *My Xx Book* to you, reward the child with an award. Copy and cut out the one shown here. Pin the award to the child's clothes.

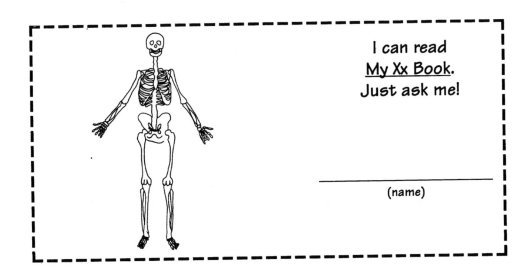

I can read
<u>My Xx Book</u>.
Just ask me!

_____
(name)

<u>CONCLUSION OF LESSON</u>

Remind the child to leave the award on until a grown-up at home asks him/her to read the book.

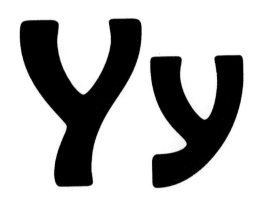

LETTER Yy

LESSON 1

Objective:

Child will

- visually recognize letter by name.
- recognize the sound /y/ in the initial position by naming words with y in that position.

Materials:

- Large chart with poem, *My Yo-Yo* (see directions on p. x)
- Any alphabet card with the letter Yy
- Letter Yy can, containing such items as:
  - yo-yo
  - yogurt container
  - yellow crayon
  - yellow paper
  - yarn

Procedure:

STEP 1

1. Introduce the lesson with the poem, *My Yo-Yo.*
2. Display the poem on an easel. You read the poem modeling 1-1 match with a pointer.

467

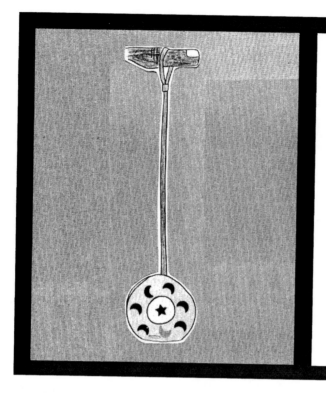

My Yo-Yo

My yo-yo can go
up and down,
up and down.
I can spin it all around!
Walk the dog
and rock the cradle,
Are tricks I can do.
Will you get a yo-yo,
And play with me too?

3. Ask the whole group, "What letter of the alphabet do you think we are studying now?"
4. Ask children to echo read the poem several times.
5. Ask children for suggestions of movements for acting out the poem.
6. Reread the poem together, acting it out!
7. Put the poem aside.

STEP 2

1. Display the alphabet card with the letter Yy.
2. Ask children to name the letter they see on the alphabet card.
3. Hold up the letter Yy can.
4. Ask children to predict what would make sense in a Yy can.
5. Take each object/picture out of the can. Name them.
6. Ask children to repeat the name of each object/picture after you name it.
7. Show children a sample of the art activity.

8. You now do the art activity with the children, either as a small group or whole class.

ART ACTIVITY

Sequin Yo-Yo's

Materials:

▪ Blackline master of poem *My Yo-Yo*
▪ Blackline master of yo-yo
▪ Crayons—multicultural and assorted colors
▪ Orange construction paper 6″ × 9″
▪ Scissors
▪ Sequins
▪ Stapler

Preparation:

Reproduce the poem *My Yo-Yo* and staple it to the right side of the orange construction paper.

Procedure:

1. Children color the finger with multicultural crayons and the yo-yo with assorted colored crayons.
2. With teacher guidance, glue and sequin the yo-yo.
3. Let dry.
4. With teacher guidance, cut out.
5. Staple yo-yo to left side of the orange construction paper.
6. Send the poem and art activity home. This gives family members an opportunity to reread the poem with the child, reinforcing the letter Yy.

CONCLUSION OF LESSON

Remind children they have learned to recognize letter Yy and they can think of words that have Yy in the initial position.

My Yo-Yo

My yo-yo can go

up and down,

up and down.

I can spin it all around!

Walk the dog,

and rock the cradle,

Are tricks I can do.

Will you get a yo-yo,

And play with me, too?

My Yo-Yo

My yo-yo can go

up and down,

up and down.

I can spin it all around!

Walk the dog,

and rock the cradle,

Are tricks I can do.

Will you get a yo-yo,

And play with me, too?

©1995 by Roberts Scoboro Press

BLACKLINE MASTER—POEM

LESSON 2

Objective:

Children will read *My Yy Book* using 1-1 match.

Materials:

- Big Book—*My Yy Book* (see directions p. xi)
- Large poem—*My Yo-Yo* (see directions p. x)
- Little books—*My Yy Book* (see directions p. xi)
- Crayons

Procedure:

1. Introduce the lesson with the poem *My Yo-Yo.*
2. You reread the poem *My Yo-Yo* modeling 1-1 match with a pointer. Children echo read the poem and act it out.
3. You hold up the "big book," *My Yy Book.* You read the title. Children echo read.
4. You go through each page of the "big book," covering all print. You name the picture on the page. Tell the children to listen for Yy words.
5. You read through the "big book" one time, modeling 1-1 match and directionality.
6. Invite the children to now read the "big book" with you. Model 1-1 match and directionality while reading.
7. The children read through the book a third time while you point to the words.

INDEPENDENT ACTIVITY

1. Reproduce blackline master of the little *My Yy Book.* Give children their own little *My Yy Book* and have them color it in. On the last page of their book, have the children draw a food they really like. You write the word on the line provided.
2. After children color in their own little *My Yy Book,* they read their book to a partner.
3. You monitor the activity, looking for 1-1 match and directionality.
4. Collect the books.

CONCLUSION OF LESSON

1. You gather the whole group back together for whole group instruction.
2. Everyone rereads the "big book," *My Yy Book,* together.
3. While the children are reading the "big book," you model 1-1 match and directionality, while pointing to the words.

My Yy Book

_____

(name)

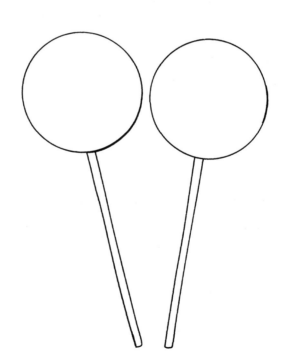

Do you like lollipops? Yes!

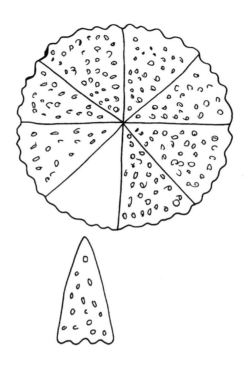

Do you like pizza? Yes!

- -

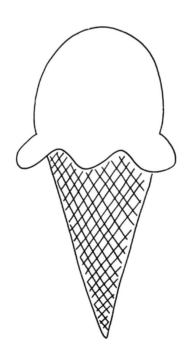

Do you like ice cream? Yes!

Do you like cookies? Yes!

Do you like _____?
Yes! Yum!

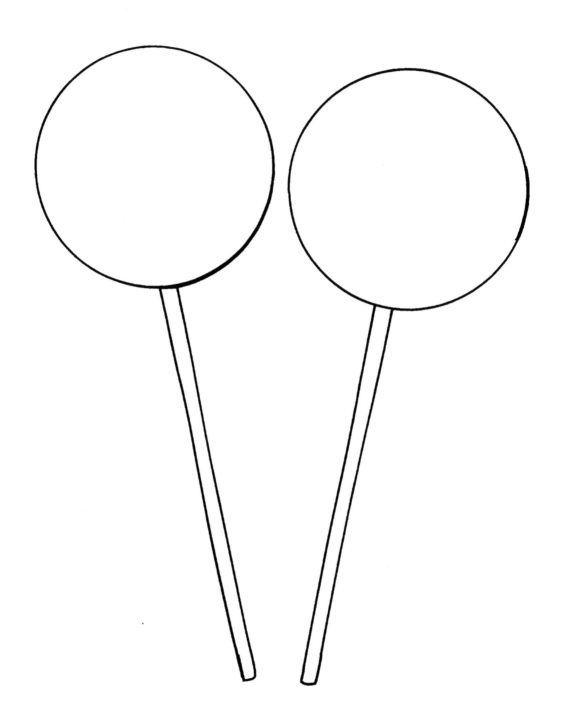

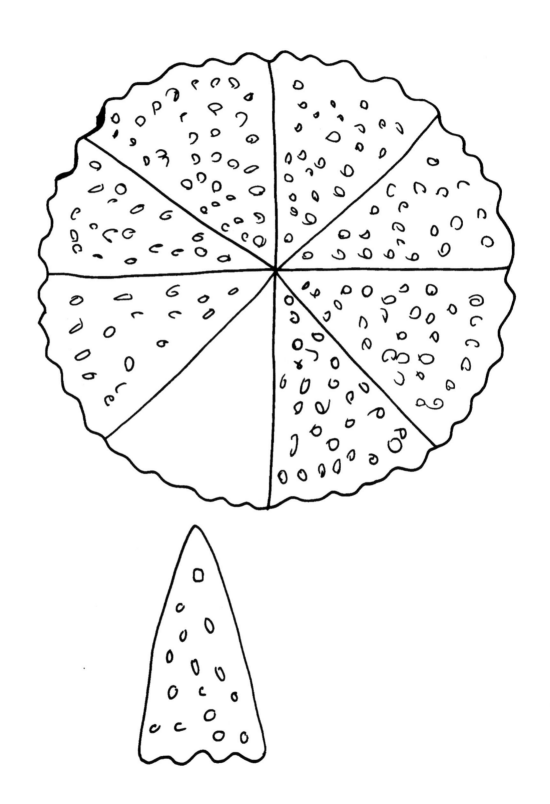

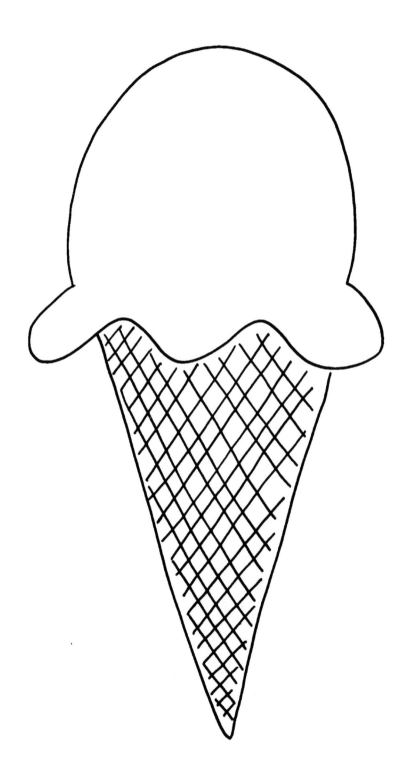

LESSON 3

Objective:

Child will focus on the 4 main cueing systems while reading little book, *My Yy Book.*

Materials:

- Big Book—*My Yy Book*
- Little books—*My Yy Book*
- Awards (see directions p. xii)
- Safety pins

Procedure:

1. Introduce the lesson with the "big book," *My Yy Book.*
2. You read the "big book" with the children, modeling 1-1 match and directionality while pointing to the words.
3. Echo read the book.

INDIVIDUALIZED INSTRUCTION

Note—The objective is to focus the child on the 4 main cueing systems:

- Meaning
- Visual
- Structure
- 1-1 Match

(See page viii for definition and more information.)

1. You now take each child, one at a time, having him/her read the little book, *My Yy Book,* to you. Child points to words while reading.
2. As the child is reading to you, you are listening for misread text and prompting the child with the appropriate question to help him/her correct the error. Your phrasing of the questions must be consistent with those in the "Examples of Misread Text."
3. Through repeated use of these techniques, the children will begin to ask themselves these questions. This indicates the child is now monitoring his/her own reading and is on the way to becoming an independent reader.
4. Following are specific examples of misread text by a child using little *My Yy Book.* Find the type of example that matches what your student has

read. After using the appropriate strategy questions and the child still cannot recall the word, then tell the child the word! Teach the child right from the start that reading is *not* a trick!

5. The child's response may not be an exact match to the example. However, if the response is a similar mistake, prompt the child with the appropriate question.

Examples of Misread Text

Following are specific examples of misread text by a child using little *My Yy Book*. Find the type of example that matches what your student has read. Keep in mind that the child's response may not be an exact match to the example. However, if the response is a similar mistake, prompt the child with the appropriate question.

WHEN TO USE MEANING QUESTIONS

Objective:

Child must determine if what he/she has read makes sense in relation to the picture and in the context of the book he/she is reading.

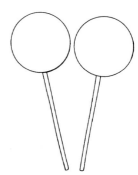

Example

Child reads:	Do you like balloons? Yes!
Text reads:	Do you like lollipops? Yes!

Strategy

Teacher:	"Look at the picture. Does balloons make sense in a book about food you like?"
Child:	"No."
Teacher:	"Good! *Good readers reread.*"

WHEN TO USE STRUCTURE QUESTIONS

Objective:

Child must be able to hear what he/she has read and determine if it sounds right grammatically.

Example

Child reads: Does you like ice cream?
Text reads: Do you like ice cream? Yes!

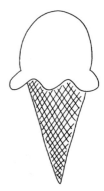

Strategy

Teacher: "Does that sound right? Is that how people talk?"

Child: "No."

Teacher: "What would sound right?"

Child: "Do you like ice cream?"

Teacher: "Good! *Good readers reread.*"

WHEN TO USE VISUAL QUESTIONS

Objective:

Child will use letter in the initial position to read a word in context.

Example

Child reads: Do you like pizza? No!
Text reads: Do you like pizza? Yes!

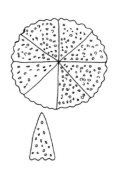

Strategy

You point to the misread word: "What word do you know starts with letter y and makes sense?"

Child: "Yes."

Teacher: "Reread."

Child: "Do you like pizza? Yes!"

If the child hesitates and cannot recall the word, give it! Then have the child reread.

WHEN TO USE 1-1 QUESTIONS

Objective:

Child must understand what he/she says has to match the number of words on the page.

Example 1

Child reads: Do you like chocolate chip cookies? Yes!
Text reads: Do you like cookies? Yes!

Strategy

Teacher: "Did your finger match the words?"

Child: "No."

Teacher: "Reread."

If the finger does not match the second time, you take the child's finger and point to the words together.

Example 2

Child reads: Do you like _____? Yes!
Text reads: Do you like _____? Yes! Yum!

Strategy

Teacher: "Did your finger match the words?"

Child: "No."

Teacher: "Reread."

If the child responds, "Yes, my finger did match," take the child's finger and point to the words together.

LETTER Yy AWARD

When the child has successfully read his/her own *My Yy Book* to you, reward the child with an award. Copy and cut out the one shown here. Pin the award to the child's clothes.

I can read
My Yy Book.
Just ask me!

_____

(name)

<u>CONCLUSION OF LESSON</u>

Remind the child to leave the award on until a grown-up at home asks him/her to read the book.

LETTER Zz

LESSON 1

Objective:

Child will

▌ visually recognize letter by name.

▌ recognize the sound /z/ in the initial position by naming words with z in that position.

Materials:

▌ Large chart with poem, *The Zoo* (see directions on p. x)

▌ Any alphabet card with the letter Zz

▌ Letter Zz can, containing such items as:
   - magazine picture of zebra
   - zipper
   - plastic zoo animals
   - number zero

Procedure:

STEP 1

1. Introduce the lesson with the poem, *The Zoo.*

2. Display the poem on an easel. You read the poem modeling 1-1 match with a pointer.

The Zoo

At the zoo you will see,
Animals from A to Z!
Alligators, elephants, monkeys too—
All doing tricks for me and you!

3. Ask the whole group, "What letter of the alphabet do you think we are studying now?"
4. Ask children to echo read the poem several times.
5. Ask children for suggestions of movements for acting out the poem.
6. Reread the poem together, acting it out!
7. Put the poem aside.

STEP 2

1. Display the alphabet card with the letter Zz.
2. Ask children to name the letter they see on the alphabet card.
3. Hold up the letter Zz can.
4. Ask children to predict what would make sense in a Zz can.
5. Take each object/picture out of the can. Name them.
6. Ask children to repeat the name of each object/picture after you name it.
7. Show children a sample of the art activity.
8. You now do the art activity with the children, either as a small group or whole class.

ART ACTIVITY

At the Zoo

Materials:

- Blackline master of poem *The Zoo*
- Blackline master of zoo animals
- Crayons
- Scissors
- Blue construction paper 12″ × 18″
- Yarn
- Hole punch
- Scotch tape
- Stapler

Preparation:

Reproduce the poem *The Zoo* and staple it to the right side of the blue construction paper. 1″ down from the top and 1″ up from the bottom, punch 6 holes, 2″ apart. Precut 6 - 12″ lengths of yarn for each child.

Procedure:

1. Children color blackline of animals.
2. Children cut out and glue on to the left side of the blue construction paper.
3. Children thread yarn vertically through the holes.
4. On the back of the paper, students (with teacher guidance, as appropriate), tape the yarn so it does not fall out of the holes.
5. Send the poem and art activity home. This gives family members an opportunity to reread the poem with the child, reinforcing the letter Zz.

CONCLUSION OF LESSON

Remind children they have learned to recognize letter Zz and they can think of words that have Zz in the initial position.

The Zoo

At the zoo,

You will see,

Animals from A to Z!

Alligators, elephants, monkeys,

too—

All doing tricks,

for me and you!

The Zoo

At the zoo,

You will see,

Animals from A to Z!

Alligators, elephants, monkeys,

too—

All doing tricks,

for me and you!

BLACKLINE MASTER—POEM

LESSON 2

Objective:

Children will read *My Zz Book* using 1-1 match.

Materials:

- Big Book—*My Zz Book* (see directions p. xi)
- Large poem—*The Zoo* (see directions p. x)
- Little books—*My Zz Book* (see directions p. xi)
- Crayons

Procedure:

1. Introduce the lesson with the poem *The Zoo.*
2. You reread the poem *The Zoo* modeling 1-1 match with a pointer. Children echo read the poem and act it out.
3. You hold up the "big book," *My Zz Book.* You read the title. Children echo read.
4. You go through each page of the "big book," covering all print. You name the picture on the page. Tell the children to listen for Zz words.
5. You read through the "big book" one time, modeling 1-1 match and directionality.
6. Invite the children to now read the "big book" with you. Model 1-1 match and directionality while reading.
7. The children read through the book a third time while you point to the words.

INDEPENDENT ACTIVITY

1. Reproduce blackline master of the little *My Zz Book.* Give children their own little *My Zz Book* and have them color it in.
2. After children color in their own little *My Zz Book,* they read their book to a partner.
3. You monitor the activity, looking for 1-1 match and directionality.
4. Collect the books.

CONCLUSION OF LESSON

1. You gather the whole group back together for whole group instruction.
2. Everyone rereads the "big book," *My Zz Book,* together.
3. While the children are reading the "big book," you model 1-1 match and directionality, while pointing to the words.

My Zz Book

_____

(name)

- -

"Zzz," said the dog.

"Zzz," said the pig.

- -

"Zzz," said the cat.

"Zzz," said the fish.

- -

"Wake up!" I said.
And they did.

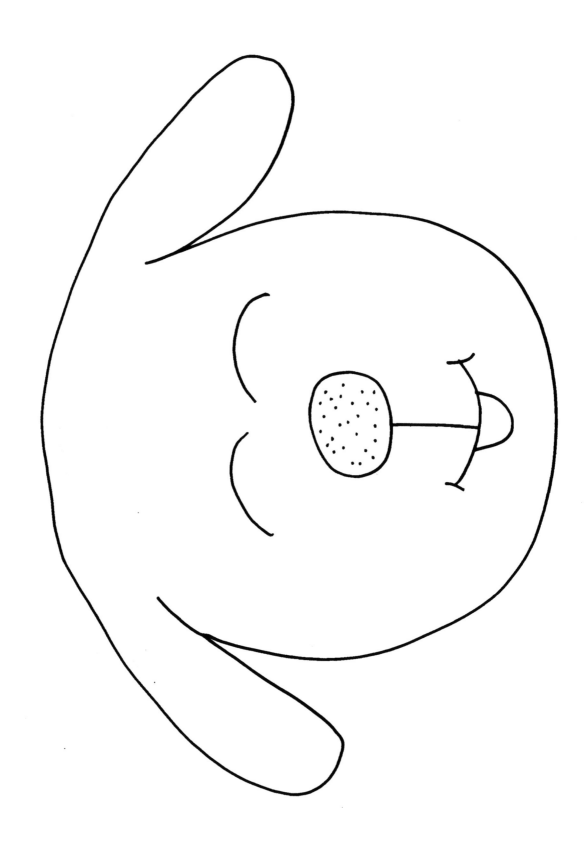

LESSON 3

Objective:

Child will focus on the 4 main cueing systems while reading little book, *My Zz Book.*

Materials:

▌ Big Book—*My Zz Book*

▌ Little books—*My Zz Book*

▌ Awards (see directions p. xii)

▌ Safety pins

Procedure:

1. Introduce the lesson with the "big book," *My Zz Book.*
2. You read the "big book" with the children, modeling 1-1 match and directionality while pointing to the words.
3. Echo read the book.

INDIVIDUALIZED INSTRUCTION

Note—The objective is to focus the child on the 4 main cueing systems:

▌ Meaning

▌ Visual

▌ Structure

▌ 1-1 Match

(See page viii for definition and more information.)

1. You now take each child, one at a time, having him/her read the little book, *My Zz Book,* to you. Child points to words while reading.
2. As the child is reading to you, you are listening for misread text and prompting the child with the appropriate question to help him/her correct the error. Your phrasing of the questions must be consistent with those in the "Examples of Misread Text."
3. Through repeated use of these techniques, the children will begin to ask themselves these questions. This indicates the child is now monitoring his/her own reading and is on the way to becoming an independent reader.
4. Following are specific examples of misread text by a child using little *My Zz Book.* Find the type of example that matches what your student has read. After using the appropriate strategy questions and the child still

cannot recall the word, then tell the child the word! Teach the child right from the start that reading is *not* a trick!

5. The child's response may not be an exact match to the example. However, if the response is a similar mistake, prompt the child with the appropriate question.

Examples of Misread Text

Following are specific examples of misread text by a child using little *My Zz Book*. Find the type of example that matches what your student has read. Keep in mind that the child's response may not be an exact match to the example. However, if the response is a similar mistake, prompt the child with the appropriate question.

WHEN TO USE MEANING QUESTIONS

Objective:

Child must determine if what he/she has read makes sense in relation to the picture and in the context of the book he/she is reading.

Example

Child reads: "Hello," said the dog.
Text reads: "Zzz," said the dog.

Strategy

Teacher:	"Does hello make sense? The dog is sleeping."
Child:	"No."
Teacher:	"What else could you try?"
Child:	"Zzzz."
Teacher:	"Good! Zzzz makes sense. *Good readers reread.*"

WHEN TO USE STRUCTURE QUESTIONS

Objective:

Child must be able to hear what he/she has read and determine if it sounds right grammatically.

Example

Child reads:	"Zzz," and the fish.
Text reads:	"Zzz," said the fish.

Strategy

Teacher:	"Does that sound right? Is that how people talk?"
Child:	"No."
Teacher:	"What would sound right?"
Child:	"Zzz, said the fish."
Teacher:	"Good! *Good readers reread."*

WHEN TO USE VISUAL QUESTIONS

Objective:

Child will use letter in the initial position to read a word in context.

Example

Child reads:	"Grr," said the dog.
Text reads:	"Zzz," said the dog.

Strategy

You point to the misread word: "What sound does the letter z make?"

Child:	"Zzzz."
Teacher:	"Reread."
Child:	"Zzzz, said the dog."

If the child hesitates and cannot recall the word, give it! Then have the child reread.

WHEN TO USE 1-1 QUESTIONS

Objective:

Child must understand what he/she says has to match the number of words on the page.

Example 1

Child reads: "Zzz," said the fat pig.
Text reads: "Zzz," said the pig.

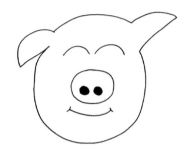

Strategy

Teacher: "Did your finger match the words?"

Child: "No."

Teacher: "Reread."

If the finger does not match the second time, you take the child's finger and point to the words together.

Example 2

Child reads: "Zzz," said cat.
Text reads: "Zzz," said the cat.

Strategy

Teacher: "Did your finger match the words?"

Child: "No."

Teacher: "Reread."

If the child responds, "Yes, my finger did match," take the child's finger and point to the words together.

LETTER Zz AWARD

When the child has successfully read his/her own *My Zz Book* to you, reward the child with an award. Copy and cut out the one shown here. Pin the award to the child's clothes.

I can read
<u>My Zz Book</u>.
Just ask me!

_____
(name)

<u>CONCLUSION OF LESSON</u>

Remind the child to leave the award on until a grown-up at home asks him/her to read the book.

Final Activity

Objective:

Children are celebrating the conclusion of their study of the alphabet.

Materials:

Large chart with poem, *The Alphabet* (see directions on p. x)

Procedure:

1. Introduce the lesson with the poem, *The Alphabet.*
2. Display the poem on an easel. You read the poem modeling 1-1 match with a pointer.

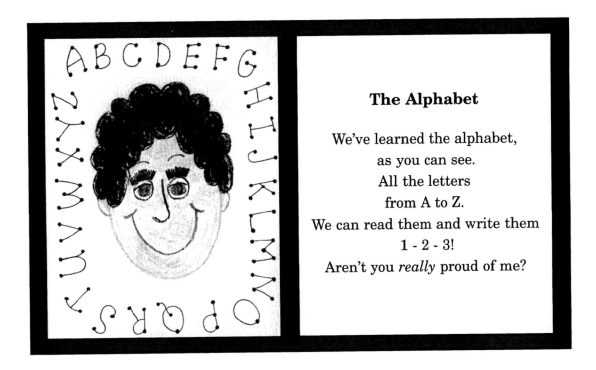

The Alphabet

We've learned the alphabet,
as you can see.
All the letters
from A to Z.
We can read them and write them
1 - 2 - 3!
Aren't you *really* proud of me?

3. Ask children to echo read the poem several times.
4. Reread the poem together.
5. Put the poem aside.
6. Show children a sample of the art activity.
7. You now do the art activity with the children, either as a small group or whole class.

ART ACTIVITY

Self-Portrait

Materials:

- Blackline master of poem *The Alphabet*
- Blackline master of self-portrait "A-Z frame"
- Crayons—multicultural and assorted colors
- Red construction paper 12" × 18"
- Stapler

Preparation:

Reproduce the poem *The Alphabet* and staple it to the right side of the red construction paper.

Procedure:

1. Children draw a self-portrait in the A-Z frame.
2. Staple portrait to left side of the red construction paper.
3. Send the poem and art activity home. This gives family members an opportunity to reread the poem with their children, celebrating the completion of their study of the alphabet.

CONCLUSION OF LESSON

Remind children they have learned all of the letters and sounds of the alphabet. Remind them to go back and reread all of their "little letter books" from time to time.

The Alphabet

We've learned the alphabet,

As you can see.

All the letters,

from A to Z!

We can read and write them

1 - 2 - 3 - !

Aren't you *really* proud of me?

- -

The Alphabet

We've learned the alphabet,

As you can see.

All the letters,

from A to Z!

We can read and write them

1 - 2 - 3 - !

Aren't you *really* proud of me?

BLACKLINE MASTER—POEM

BLACKLINE MASTER—ALPHABET FRAME

Bibliography

Aa

I Want to Be an Astronaut, Byron Barton. Thomas Y. Crowell Co., 1988.

The Armadillo from Amarillo, Lynne Cherry. Harcourt Brace Jovanovich, 1994.

Arthur's Birthday, Marc Brown. Little, Brown & Co, 1989.

Ten Apples Up on Top, Theo LeSieg. Beginner Books, 1961.

There's an Alligator Under My Bed, Mercer Mayer. Dial Books for Young Readers, 1987.

Bb

Brown Bear Brown Bear What Do You See? Bill Martin, Jr. Holt, Rinehart & Winston, 1970.

Wheels on the Bus, Maryann Kovalski. Little, Brown & Co., 1987.

Little Bear, Else Holmelund Minark. Harper & Row, 1968.

The Big Block of Chocolate, Janet Slater Redhead. Scholastic Inc., 1985.

Barney Bipple's Magic Dandelions, Carol Chapman. E.P. Dutton, 1977.

Cc

Hello, Cat You Need a Hat, Rita Golden Gelman. Scholastic Inc., 1979.

Have You Seen the Crocodile?, Colin West. Harper & Row, 1986.

The Mixed-Up Chameleon, Eric Carle. Harper & Row, 1975.

The Carrot Seed, Ruth Krauss. Scholastic Inc., 1945.

Corduroy, Don Freeman. Viking Press, 1968.

Millions of Cats, Wanda Ga'g. Scholastic Inc., 1986.

Dd

I Wish That I Had Duck Feet, Theo LeSieg. Random House Inc., 1965.

Duckat, Gaelyn Gordon. Scholastic Inc., 1992.

There's No Such Thing as a Dragon, Jack Kent. Western Publishing Co. Inc., 1975.

Dandelion, Don Freeman. Puffin Books, 1964.

The Dinosaur Egg Mystery, Val Biro. Barron's Education Series Inc., 1992.

Harry the Dirty Dog, Gene Zion. Harper & Row, 1956.

Ee

The Ear Book, Al Perkins. Random House, Inc., 1968.

The Elephant and the Bad Baby, Elfrida Vipont & Raymond Briggs. Coward-McCann, Inc., 1969.

Elephant in Trouble, Thomas Crawford. Troll Associates, 1970.

The Right Number of Elephants, Jeff Sheppard. Scholastic Inc., 1990.

Ernst, Elisa Kleven. E.P. Dutton, 1989.

Ff

The Rainbow Fish, Marcus Pfister. Scholastic Inc., 1992.

Firehouse Dog, Amy and Richard Hutchings. Scholastic Inc., 1993.

We Are Best Friends, Alike. Mulberry Books, 1982.

Franklin Fibs, Paulette Buorgeois. Scholastic Inc., 1991.

Franklin in the Dark, Paulette Buorgeois. Scholastic Inc., 1986.

Felix the Funny Fox, Ski Michaels. Troll Associates, 1986.

Gg

Gregory, the Terrible Eater, Mitchell Sharmat. Scholastic Inc., 1980.

Billy Goats Gruff, Pat McKissack. Children's Press, 1987.

The Giving Tree, Shel Silverstein. Harper Collins, 1964.

When I Grow Up, Heidi Coennel. Little, Brown & Co., 1987.

The Gorilla Did It, Barbara Shook Hazen. Atheneum, 1974.

Hh

There's a Hippopotamus Under My Bed, Mike Thaler. Avon Camelot, 1978.

Up the Haystack, Sally Moss. Scholastic Inc., 1987.

A House Is a House for Me, Mary Ann Hoberman. Viking Press, 1978.

"You Look Ridiculous" Said the Rhinoceros to the Hippopotamus, Bernard Waber. Houghton Mifflin, 1966.

The Happy Hippopotami, Bill Martin, Jr. Harcourt Brace Jovanovich, 1970.

Howard, James Stevenson. Greenwillow Books, 1980.

Ii

Itchy, Itchy Chicken Pox, Grace Maccarone. Scholastic Inc., 1992.

I Was Walking Down the Road, Sarah E. Barchas. Scholastic Inc., 1975.

Ice Cream Soup, Frank Modell. Greenwillow, 1988.

The Igloo, Charlotte Yue. Houghton Mifflin Co., 1988.

The Little Island, Golden MacDonald and Leonard Weisgard. Doubleday, 1946.

The Itchy Witch, Janet Slater Redhead. Wright Group, 1985.

Jj

Jump Frog Jump, Robert Kalan. Scholastic Inc., 1981.

Jamberry, Bruce Degen. Harper & Row, 1983.

Jessica, Kevin Henkes. Greenwillow Books, 1989.

Jillian Jiggs, Phoebe Gilman. Scholastic Inc., 1985.

The Day Jimmy's Boa Ate the Wash, Trinka Hakes Noble. Scholastic Inc., 1980.

Joey, Jack Kent. Prentice-Hall, 1984.

Kk

Katy No-Pocket, Emmy Payne. Houghton Mifflin Co., 1944.

Bringing the Rain to Kapiti Plain, Verna Aardema. Scholastic Inc., 1981.

What Would You Do with a Kangaroo?, Mercer Mayer. Scholastic Inc., 1973.

But Not Kate, Marissa Moss. Lothrop, Lee & Shepard, 1992.

Ll

There Was an Old Lady, Unknown. Child's Play, 1973.

Snow Lion, David McPhail. *Parent's Magazine* Press, 1982.

Ladybug Ladybug, Ruth Brown. Dutton Children's Books, 1988.

Mamma Do You Love Me?, Barbara M. Joose. Chronicle Books, 1991.

Lyle Lyle Crocodile, Bernard Waber. Houghton Mifflin, 1965.

Mm

If You Give a Moose a Muffin, Laura Joffe Numeroff. Harper Collins, 1991.

The Mystery of the Missing Red Mitten, Steven Kellog. Dial Books, 1974.

The Cake That Mack Ate, Rose Robart. Little Brown & Co., 1986.

One Hungry Monster, Susan Heyboer O'Keefe. Joy Street/Little Brown, & Co., 1989.

Seven Little Monsters, Maurice Sendak. Harper & Row, 1975.

Mop Top, Don Freeman. Puffin Books, 1955.

Nn

Noisy Nora, Rosemary Wells. Scholastic Inc., 1973.

The Napping House, Audrey Wood. Harcourt Brace Jovanovich, 1984.

The Best Nest, P.D. Eastman. Random House, 1968.

Nathan's Fishing Trip, Lulu Delacre. Scholastic Inc., 1988.

All of Our Noises Are Here, Alvin Schwartz. Harper & Row, 1985.

Oo

My Very Own Octopus, Bernard Most. Harcourt Brace Jovanovich, 1980.

Owen, Kevin Henkes. Greenwillow Books, 1993.

Otto Is Different, Franz Brandenberg. Greenwillow Books, 1985.

Good-Night Owl, Pat Hutchins. Macmillan Publishing Co., 1972.

One Hundred Hungry Ants, Elinor J. Pinczes. Houghton Mifflin, 1993.

One Gorilla, Atsuko Morozumi. Farrar, Straus & Giroux, 1990.

Pp

Polar Express, Chris Van Allsburg. Houghton-Mifflin, 1985.

Little Penguins Tale, Audrey Wood. Scholastic Inc., 1989.

Picking Peas for a Penny, Angela Shelf Medearis. Scholastic Inc., 1990.

Pig Pig Grows Up, David McPhail. E.P. Dutton, 1980.

Pancakes Pancakes, Eric Carle. Scholastic Inc., 1990.

Peter's Pockets, Eve Rice. Greenwillow Books, 1989.

Qq

The Quilt Story, Tony Johnston. G.P. Putnam & Sons, 1985.

Sam Johnson and the Blue Ribbon Quilt, Lisa Campbell Ernst. Mulberry Books, 1983.

The Patchwork Quilt, Valerie Flournoy. Penguin Books, 1985.

Quail Song, Valerie Carey. G. P. Putnam & Sons, 1990.

The Quiet Noise Book, Margaret Wise Brown. Harper Collins, 1950.

Rr

Rosie's Walk, Pat Hutchins. Macmillan Publishing Co., 1968.

Ruby the Copycat, Peggy Rathmann. Scholastic Inc., 1991.

A Rainbow of My Own, Don Freeman. Penguin Books, 1987.

Harold's Runaway Nose, Harriet Sonnenschein. Simon & Schuster, 1989.

Mr. Rabbit and the Lovely Present, Charlotte Zolotow. Harper & Row, 1977.

Roll Over, Unknown. Houghton Mifflin/Clarion Books, 1969.

Ss

Stone Soup, Ann McGovern. Scholastic Inc., 1986.

Slugs, David Greenberg. Little, Brown & Co., 1983.

Strega Nona, Tomie de Paola. Scholastic Inc., 1975.

The Tiny Seed, Eric Carle. Scholastic Inc., 1989.

Something Special, David McPhail. Little, Brown & Co., 1988.

And I Mean It Stanley, Crosby Bonsall. Harper & Row, 1974.

Tt

10 for Dinner, Jo Ellen Bogart. Scholastic Inc., 1989.

The Trip, Ezra Jack Keats. Scholastic Inc., 1978.

Today Was a Terrible Day, Patricia Reilly Giff. Penguin Group, 1984.

Tacky the Penguin, Helen Lester. Houghton Mifflin, 1988.

Who Wants an Old Teddy Bear?, Ginnie Hofman. Random House Inc., 1978.

Who Is Tapping at My Window?, A.G. Deming. E.P. Dutton, 1988.

Uu

Umbrella, Taro Yashima. Viking Press, 1958.

Under Your Feet, Joanne Ryder. Macmillan, 1990.

Vv

Emma's Vacation, David McPhail. Dutton, 1987.

Arthur's Valentine, Marc Brown. Avon, 1980.

Growing Vegetable Soup, Lois Ehlert. Harcourt Brace Jovanovich, 1987.

Mountains and Volcanoes, Eileen Curran. Troll Associates, 1985.

Vegetable Garden, Douglas Florian. Harcourt Brace Jovanovich, 1991.

Arthur's Family Vacation, Marc Brown. Little, Brown & Co., 1993.

Ww

The Wolf's Chicken Stew, Keiko Kasza. G.P. Putnam & Sons, 1987.

Mrs. Wishy-Washy, Joy Cowley. Wright Group, 1990.

Who Sank the Boat?, Pamela Allen. Coward-McCann Inc., 1982.

Humphrey the Lost Whale, Wendy Tokuda. Heran International Inc., 1989.

Where Have You Been?, Margaret Wise Brown. Scholastic Inc., 1984.

Xx

Skeletons! Skeletons! All About Bones, Katy Hall. Scholastic Inc., 1991.

Yy

Yellow Yellow, Frank Asch. McGraw-Hill, 1971.

My Time of Year, Katherine Dow. Henry Z. Walck, Inc., 1961.

Zz

A Visit to the Zoo, Sylvia Root Tester. Children's Press, 1987.

Dear Zoo, Rod Campbell. Puffin Books, 1982.

If I Ran the Zoo, Dr. Seuss. Random House, 1950.

Zoo, Where Are You?, Ann McGovern. Harper, 1964.

Mrs. Toggle's Zipper, Robin Pulver. Macmillan, 1993.

Greedy Zebra, Mwenye Hadithi. Little, Brown & Co., 1984.

Notes

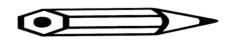

Notes